OVERSIGHT

How To Build Leadership Architecture So Your Business No Longer Owns You.

Joe Papadatos

ISBN: 978-1-7644786-0-1

Imprint: Independently published

For permission requests, contact: joe@twoicons.com.au

ISBN: 978-1-7644786-0-1

First published in Australia in 2026.

Independently published.

Edited by Katherine Lewis.

Disclaimer

The information in this book is based on the author's personal experience and professional observations. It is intended for general informational and educational purposes only. This book does not constitute, and should not be relied upon as, financial, legal, psychological, or business advisory services.

Results described in case studies reflect individual circumstances and are not guaranteed. All case studies use pseudonyms and altered details to protect privacy; any resemblance to specific individuals or businesses is coincidental.

Readers are encouraged to seek qualified professional advice for their specific circumstances. The author and publisher disclaim liability for any actions taken based on the contents of this book.

This book discusses mental health topics including founder burnout, depression, and suicidal ideation for informational purposes only. It is not a substitute for professional mental health support. If you or someone you know is experiencing a mental health crisis, please contact Lifeline on 13 11 14 or Beyond Blue on 1300 22 4636 in Australia, or your local crisis service.

Dedication

To my daughters – Rebecca, Renee, and Ellie – you saw the late nights, the missed moments, the pressure I carried home. You worked alongside me. This book is for you, and for every founder's child who knows what that costs.

Contents

Foreword

I worked with Joe Papadatos for more than eight years, so I got to see a lot. I was there when Icon Visual Marketing announced itself as the largest agency in Southwest Sydney. The growth, the client wins, the accounts and relationships that lasted for years. From the outside, it looked like everything was humming.

From the inside, though, I saw what it actually took to keep the momentum going. Yes Joe owned the business but he carried a lot, much more than he should have at the time. Every big decision, every problem that landed. Icon consumed his waking hours, his energy, and his family life. He held the whole thing together through sheer determination, and for a long time, that's how it worked.

What I didn't fully appreciate, until much later, was what that cost him and those of us within the business. We weren't a team that lacked capability, Icon attracted many talented, passionate people. However somewhere along the way, we all expected Joe to have the answer for everything. When things got tricky, we'd escalate. When we weren't sure, we'd defer for direction. We weren't doing it consciously, it had just become the rhythm of the place. Joe, to his credit (and perhaps his detriment), was always there to catch whatever came his way.

Then things started to change. It wasn't dramatic or sudden it was gradual. But it was real and it had an impact on the way we working on a daily basis. Clearer agreements started to appear around who owned what, with genuine accountability. Regular rhythms and check-ins meant problems got caught early, before they had a chance to grow into something bigger. We began collaborating more across functions, and slowly, space opened up for the rest of us to step into. Which also meant space for Joe to step back, something that didn't always come naturally to him.

I won't pretend it worked straight away. We were so used to Joe being at the centre of everything, and he was too. It took some adjusting. We stumbled along the way but we always leant from it.

Our clients needed to adjust too, Joe was the centre of the business and they would often ask 'what does Joe think'. His opinion has always mattered.

Then we found our stride. We started owning outcomes rather than just completing tasks. We started making calls without needing to check in first. The business didn't fall apart without Joe holding it all together. If anything, it found a steadier kind of strength.

What's in this book is essentially the thinking behind all of that. The structure Joe built, piece by piece, bringing us along on the journey. I lived inside it. I watched it take shape and I can say with confidence that it works.

If you're a founder who's been carrying more than your share, who somehow became the glue holding everything together and isn't quite sure how that happened, this book is worth your time. There is another way.

I know, because I watched someone figure it out.

Nicole Smith

Head of Client Services

Icon Visual Marketing (2015–2023)

Introduction

You've picked up this book because you're successful but you're also drowning.

Revenue's growing. Your team's expanding. Clients are happy. But you're spent, wondering how much longer you can keep going like this.

Every decision still flows through you. Every problem somehow lands on your desk. The gaps in the system? You fill them. With your time. Your energy. Your weekends.

You tell yourself this is what leadership looks like. But it's not. It's a trap, one you built with your own hands. Not because you're bad at delegation. Because you built something that can't hold without you filling every gap.

I've watched too many founders lose themselves to businesses that didn't need the sacrifice. I was one of them. And I learned the hard way that the burden wasn't inevitable, it was an architecture problem.

Architecture can be built.

This book is the framework I wish someone had handed me ten years earlier. What follows isn't motivation. It's a structure for founders who are done with being the glue and who are ready to build something that holds without them.

The Real Conversation

For twenty years, I ran Icon Visual Marketing with a single obsession: helping founders grow their revenue.

We built brands for property developers, retail chains, and professional services firms. That holistic view transformed Icon from a startup into Southwest Sydney's largest marketing agency.

But here's what I learned over two decades: the marketing strategies were always secondary.

Founders would come wanting to talk about lead generation, brand positioning, conversion optimisation. That's what they thought they needed.

But within ten minutes, the real conversation would emerge.

Cash flow. "Joe, we're growing, but we're always chasing payments."

Stress. "I haven't taken a real day off in eighteen months."

Staff. "My team keeps waiting for me to make every decision."

Family. "My marriage is strained. My kids barely know me. I built this business to create freedom, and now I'm more trapped than when I worked for someone else."

The pattern was always the same, regardless of industry or business size. Whether it was a 15-person consulting firm or an 80-employee manufacturing company, I heard a variation on one phrase over and over:

"I can't keep going like this."

More people didn't solve it. More revenue didn't solve it. Better marketing definitely didn't solve it.

Because the problem wasn't tactical. It was architectural.

These founders had built businesses that required them to be the glue holding everything together. And as the business grew, the glue just had to stretch further. I watched this pattern for twenty years. Hundreds of founders. Same struggle.

And then I looked in the mirror.

Icon was succeeding. Revenue was strong. Our clients were happy. But I was living the exact pattern I'd been observing.

The research on founders tells a sobering story: most report that business success has come at the expense of their personal relationships. True disconnection from the business barely exists for founders with growing teams. And the constant weight of being the "go-to person" is the primary barrier to strategic thinking for most.

This wasn't a time management problem. It wasn't a delegation problem. It wasn't even a people problem.

It was an architecture problem.

By 2023, I was emotionally worn down. Twenty years of being the engine. Twenty years of filling every gap. Twenty years of being the glue.

So I sold Icon to an international agency.

Not because it was failing. Because I was.

And that's when Oversight crystallised.

Not as a theory I invented in isolation. But as a pattern I'd seen for twenty years, in hundreds of founder conversations, as well as in my own collapse and rebuilding.

Oversight is the architecture that lets founders move from being the glue to being the Architect. This book is that blueprint.

If you're a founder of a 10–100 person business, working unsustainable hours, feeling like you're the one holding everything together, this is for you.

Because the real conversation you need to have isn't about marketing, sales, or operations.

It's about architecture.

And I've built it. Let me show you how.

You Are Not Alone: Voices of Vulnerability

Before we step into the story, know this: the burden you feel, the quiet panic, the fear that admitting exhaustion makes you weak, these are not signs of failure. They are shared by some of the most successful leaders in the world...

Arianna Huffington (Founder, Huffington Post; collapsed from burnout in 2007)

"After I collapsed and broke my cheekbone from fatigue, that was the beginning of my journey to recognise that being vulnerable and knowing when I needed to ask for help is actually a sign of strength."[1]

---

[1] Dowden, C., PhD. (2021, June 8). The Power of Vulnerability for Resilient Leadership: Insights from Arianna Huffington and Nabeela Ixtabalan. *Forbes*.
https://www.forbes.com/sites/forbesbooksauthors/2021/06/08/the-power-of-vulnerability-for-resilient-leadership-insights-from-arianna-huffington-and-nabeela-ixtabalan/

"I lost motivation. I just didn't care. I knew I cared deeply, but I had nothing left... In my burnt-out state I could not lead the company.[2]"

Katerina Schneider (Founder & CEO, Ritual)

"As a founder, I did not want people to see my vulnerabilities... But that moment of vulnerability was a huge relief for people, that they could also feel different things and express them... I think it's made our business stronger.[3]"

"Vulnerability sounds like truth and feels like courage. Truth and courage are not always comfortable, but they are never weaknesses.[4]"

You are in good company. The leaders who changed the world first admitted they could not carry it alone.

Now, let us begin the shift.

---

[2] Joel Gascoigne, Founder CEO @ Buffer. (2026, February 6). My Experience with Burnout as a Startup Founder. *Buffer.* https://buffer.com/resources/burnout/

[3] Christine Lagorio-Chafkin. (2021 December 9). Why Vulnerability Is Vital to Good Leadership. *Inc.* https://www.inc.com/magazine/202110/christine-lagorio-chafkin/ritual-katerina-schneider-vulnerable-leader-burnout-mental-health.html

[4] Brené Brown. (2012). *Daring Greatly: How the Courage to be Vulnerable Transforms the Way We Live, Love, Parent and Lead.* Hay House.

THE STORY AND THE SHIFT

How Collapse Revealed the Architecture Every Leader Needs

Before I share the Oversight framework with you, you need to understand my journey – because I bet as you read it, you'll see parallels with your own. What I learned the hard way was that I could see everyone else's challenges clearly, but I couldn't see my own.

As a founder, it's not easy to admit that you don't have all the answers. That you can't see a way to get out from under the constant pressure you're facing.

Remember though, you are not alone in feeling this way. All founders go through this.

What I'm going to share in the next three chapters are some simple reflective techniques you can use to start mapping your path forward. To see your blindspots. To notice where you are the glue.

You'll no doubt have been told by many people that you need to work ON your business, not IN it. Some of you reading this might even believe you are working ON your business more than IN it.

I'll help you see why that might not be the case. Not because you aren't trying, but because our definition as business owners of what constitutes working ON the business is often fundamentally flawed.

Only once you can see where you are the glue can you begin building the architecture that will "unstick" you from your business.

I'll also introduce you to the greatest hurdle you'll face in developing Oversight: your own mind. This is where the doubts and fears that are holding you back live.

So, consider these first chapters a mirror, held up by a loving hand.

Because only once you see your situation clearly, can you truly start to make the shift that will not only benefit you, but your whole business.

CHAPTER 1

Values Without Architecture: Love, Service, and the Gap I Couldn't See

Every leader carries a story, and mine began long before I realised what I was actually building.

Icon Visual Marketing wasn't a business; it was an expression of who I was at the time: a young founder with more heart than structure, more instinct than architecture, and a belief that if I served my team well, everything else would fall into place.

For years, that belief worked.

Our values were Love and Service. These weren't slogans on a wall. They were the way we operated.

Love meant we didn't walk away from problems or each other. It demanded transparency, not just in our systems, but in how we showed up for each other. It meant commitment to something bigger than individual success. And it meant a relentless pursuit of excellence, not perfection, but the kind of growth that comes from genuinely trying to be better.

Like a good family, Love meant learning how to serve our stakeholders, not in a mushy, feel-good way, but in practical ways that built trust, assurance, and the foundation to grow together.

Service was equally demanding. It wasn't about putting clients first. My job as the founder was to serve my team. Service meant giving, not effort, but the kind of attention and care that helped people do their best work. It meant delighting clients, yes, but also creating the conditions for the team to thrive.

We built relationships that lasted, delivered work that mattered, and created a culture where people genuinely cared about each other.

Clients stayed. Staff stayed. Growth came steadily, almost naturally, as if the values themselves were carrying us forward. But values, I would later learn, are not self-sustaining.

They are powerful, but they are also fragile. They need something to hold them, something to translate them into behaviours and rhythms that endure when pressure rises.

Culture is not a feeling. Culture is not a vibe. Culture is not a poster or a mantra.

Culture is a system.

And without architecture, even the strongest culture will drift.

The Blindspot

I spent twenty years diagnosing this pattern in others.

I could spot it in a ten-minute conversation. The weight they were carrying. The glue they'd become. The gap between what they thought was happening and what was actually happening.

I had a vocabulary for it. Tools for analysing it. Frameworks for understanding it.

I could see it in the founder who couldn't take a vacation. In the CEO whose team waited for every decision. In the business owner who built something successful and felt more trapped than ever.

I saw it hundreds of times.

And I was blind to it in myself.

For most of my career, I prided myself on being a strategist. I was someone who could see patterns, anticipate problems, and design solutions before others even noticed the cracks.

But the hardest patterns to see are the ones inside your own life. The ones you're too close to. The ones you're emotionally invested in. The ones you're responsible for.

I spent twenty years watching founders fill every gap themselves. Observing how delegation without architecture created dependency. Noticing how growth without structure created fatigue. Seeing how success without sustainability created collapse.

I could diagnose it in almost every founder I met.

But I couldn't see that Icon had all the same symptoms.

We had a leadership team. We had external advisors. We had stable clients, strong values, and systems that had grown with us over time. On paper, everything looked fine.

But beneath the surface, something was drifting.

Not catastrophically. Not visibly. Just... drifting.

Communication would scatter slightly. Decisions would take longer. People would hesitate instead of acting. And I would fill the gaps without realising I was doing it.

The pattern was always the same, in the hundreds of founders I advised, and eventually, in myself:

Delegation without architecture is hope.

And when the architecture is missing, the founder becomes the glue.

The Space Between Intention and Reality

This is what I would later come to understand as the Oversight Gap.

It's the space between what you think is happening and what is really happening. The distance between intention and execution, between clarity and assumption, between delegation and ownership.

It's the gap where leaders unconsciously become the glue, not because they want to, but because the architecture is missing.

I didn't see the Oversight Gap at first. Most leaders don't.

We see the symptoms: the frustration, the confusion, the slowdowns. The need to step in more often than we'd like.

But we don't see the gap itself. We don't see that the problem isn't the people or the workload or the market pressure. The problem is the missing architecture between what we intend and what happens. And without that architecture, we fill the gap ourselves.

We become the translators, the connectors, the clarifiers, the decision-makers, the quality controllers.

We become the system.

We become what holds everything. We become the glue.

The 3AM Questions

I started noticing the pattern in myself through the nights.

The nights got longer. I found myself awake at 3AM, staring at the ceiling, feeling the load of decisions that no one else even knew existed.

Those nights became a ritual of quiet panic, the kind of panic you can't talk about because you're the one everyone else looks to for stability.

I would reach for my phone and type questions into Google that I couldn't ask my team, my advisors, or even my spouse.

Questions like:

Why am I the only one who sees the problems?

How do I get my team to take ownership?

What happens if my best person leaves?

Will I have enough working capital?

How do I keep going when I'm drained?

These weren't business questions. They were survival questions.

And they were the exact same questions I'd heard from hundreds of founders over twenty years. These are the questions that appear when the Oversight Gap exists. When the founder is carrying weight that should be held by structure. When delegation has happened on paper, but ownership hasn't transferred in reality.

For twenty years, I'd heard these questions from others and helped them think through solutions. But when they were mine, when I was the one awake at 3AM searching for answers, I understood something I'd missed:

The pattern wasn't about working harder or hiring better people or implementing better systems.

The pattern was about architecture.

And I didn't have it.

What COVID Revealed

When COVID arrived, it didn't hit us like a single blow. It seeped in quietly, like water finding cracks you didn't know existed.

At first, it was a temporary disruption. A few weeks of uncertainty, a few adjustments to how we worked. But slowly, almost imperceptibly, the ground began to shift.

Fear crept into conversations. Anxiety replaced initiative. People who had once been confident and collaborative began to retreat into themselves.

I watched a culture that had been strong for two decades begin to wobble under the load of something none of us had ever faced.

I kept telling myself that if I worked harder, if I just held the team together a little tighter, we would get through it.

But the truth was harder to face: our culture was strong because I was holding it. And I was breaking.

The pandemic didn't create the Oversight Gap. It exposed it.

When I could no longer be physically present, when proximity disappeared as my primary management tool, the fragility of what I'd built became undeniable.

Icon looked healthy. It had strong values, a good culture, and a talented team.

But it only functioned because I was the connective tissue between everything.

And when that tissue stretched too far, when I couldn't be in every conversation and every decision, the whole thing wobbled. Not because the team wasn't capable. But because I'd never built the architecture that would allow them to be capable without me.

It took selling my business, the breakdown of my marriage, and the exhaustion of carrying too much for too long to see what had been missing all along.

Love and Service had carried us far, but they were not enough to withstand a world that had suddenly become unpredictable. They needed a structure, an architecture, that could protect them when everything else was shaking.

For twenty years, I'd been observing this pattern in others, watching founders struggle with the gap between what they delegated and what their systems could actually hold.

And I'd been living it myself without seeing it.

Until collapse forced me to see.

That's when I finally understood what I'd been missing.

That's when I discovered Oversight.

CHAPTER 2

Oversight: What It Is and What It Isn't

When I broke, I was forced to confront a word I'd dodged for years, a word that seemed weighty, corporate, and even accusatory.

I had control, but I did not have Oversight.

I had control because my hands were in everything. However, reflecting upon the situation, I recognised that the business would perform well where I performed well and poorly where I performed poorly. This indicated that the business did not provide the objective and structural Oversight required to support the expansion of the business.

For most of my life, I had associated the word "oversight" with bureaucracy, compliance, and people looking over your shoulder. "Oversight" sounded like policing. "Oversight" sounded like mistrust. "Oversight" sounded like the exact opposite of the "Culture of Love and Service" I had strived to establish.

However, the reality of collapse has a knack for tearing away illusions. It compels you to notice things you do not want to notice.

And what I finally realised was this:

Oversight does not mean control.

Oversight is clarity.

Oversight is protection.

Oversight is architecture.

What Oversight Actually Is

Here's what I actually mean by Oversight, because the word itself is part of the problem.

Oversight lets you see what's happening in your business without being in the middle of everything.

It's not surveillance. It's not micromanagement. And it's not bureaucracy disguised as "governance."

Oversight is the system of structures, rhythms, and visibility that lets the company run at a high level even when you're not the connective tissue holding it all together.

Think of it like this: when you hold everything together, you are in control by proximity. You know what's going on because you are in all the meetings, part of all the decisions, privy to all the crisis situations. You are the database that everyone checks. You are the translator between the departments. You are the quality control person who checks things before they break.

That's not leadership. That's being a very smart cog in your own machine.

Oversight is the exact opposite. Instead of being at the centre of all things, you create a structure through which you can see what's working and what's drifting. You can spot what needs fixing without being the one who must do the fixing.

Working ON vs. Working IN: What Nobody Explains

Every business book tells you to "work ON your business, not IN it."

But nobody tells you what that actually means. Most founders don't know how to tell which one they're doing. And even fewer know how to make the shift.

I thought I knew the difference for twenty years. I was wrong.

What I Thought It Meant

I thought working IN the business meant grunt work. Emails. Paperwork. Admin. And working ON the business meant strategy. Planning. Thinking. Big decisions.

So, I elevated myself. I stopped doing admin jobs. I hired people to run my operations. I concentrated on "strategy."

Client meetings? Strategic. Hiring decisions? Strategic. Planning sessions? Strategic. Problem-solving for my leadership team? Strategic.

I was working ON the business. Or so I thought.

But I was still exhausted. Still working 60-hour weeks. Still the person everyone waited for.

And I couldn't figure out why.

What It Actually Means

Here's what took me twenty years to figure out:

Working *IN* the business = *YOU* are the system.

Working *ON* the business = You're *BUILDING* a system that doesn't need you to be it.

It's not about the *TYPE* of work. It's about *WHO* the work is building.

There's a simple test you can do to find out which way you're operating right now. One question that will open your eyes to what you've been missing.

The Test: Who Gets Stronger?

After you finish something – a meeting, a decision, a crisis – ask yourself: "Who got stronger from what I did?"

If the answer is "me" → you're working IN the business.

You solved the problem. You made the decision. You handled the crisis. You maintained the relationship. The business got the outcome it needed. But it didn't get any less dependent on you.

Next time the same situation arises, it will need you again.

If the answer is "the system" → you're working ON, the business.

You built a process that handles this type of problem. You created clarity so future decisions don't need you. You developed a person who can now handle this without you. You documented the approach, so the system carries the knowledge. The business got the outcome *AND* it became less dependent on you.

Next time the same situation arises, the system handles it.

Real Example: The Client Crisis

The scenario: One of your major clients is upset. The project's three weeks behind. They're talking to competitors. The relationship is hanging by a thread.

Here's what happens when you're working IN the business (what I did for years):

I step in. I call the client personally. I smooth things over. I reassure them. I get the project back on track. I save the relationship.

Result: Client stays. Urgent situation averted. I'm the hero.

But who got stronger? Me.

The business learned: "When a client relationship is at risk, Joe fixes it."

Next time a client gets unhappy? They escalate to me.

I didn't build the business. I built my indispensability.

Now let's look at what outcome you get by working ON the business (what Oversight taught me):

I don't step in. Instead, I ask the account director who owns this client: "What do you think should happen here?"

She tells me her plan. It's good. Maybe not exactly what I would do, but it's solid.

I say: "You own this client relationship. This is yours to solve. I trust you."

She handles it. Calls the client. Gets the project back on track. Saves the relationship.

Result: Client stays. Crisis resolved. She's the hero.

But who got stronger? The system.

The business learned: "When a client relationship is at risk, the account director who owns it handles it."

The next time a client gets unhappy? The account director handles it without me.

I didn't solve the problem. I built the capability to solve problems.

Why This Is So Hard to See

The reason most founders (including me) stay stuck working IN the business while thinking they're working ON it is simple: both versions look like leadership.

In both the scenarios I've just shared, I made a judgement call. I was involved. I added value. But in one scenario, I made the business stronger. In the other, I made myself more necessary.

Here's how to tell the difference...

IN vs. ON: The Oversight Way

When you're working IN the business, you ARE the system.

Problems get solved when you solve them.

Decisions get made when you make them.

Clarity exists when you provide it.

The business functions when you function.

Growth requires more of you.

Test: If you took a week off with zero contact, what would break?

If the answer is "a lot" → you're working IN the business. YOU are the system.

By contrast, when you're working ON the business, you're BUILDING the system.

Problems get solved by processes you designed.

Decisions get made by people with clear authority.

Clarity exists in documented roles and outcomes.

The business functions because of architecture, not proximity.

Growth happens through systems, not your hours.

Test: If you took a week off with zero contact, what would break?

If the answer is "very little" → you're working ON the business. The SYSTEM is the system.

What "Working ON" Looks Like

Every business book tells you to work ON your business. None of them show you what that actually looks like in practice. Here are some tangible examples of what it looks like when you stop being the glue, step out of working IN your business and start working ON it.

Instead of: Making the decision yourself...

You do: Figure out who should be making this type of decision, give them the authority, and clarify what they should consider.

Instead of: Solving the problem...

You do: Build a process so this problem doesn't recur, or train someone to solve it.

Instead of: Answering the question...

You do: Create clarity (Role Agreement, documentation, process) so the question doesn't need to be asked.

Instead of: Stepping in when things wobble...

You do: Let the shake happen, observe what broke, strengthen the architecture.

Instead of: Being available to fill gaps...

You do: Identify what creates the gaps and build structure to eliminate them.

Instead of: Maintaining relationships personally...

You do: Develop people who own relationships and create systems that preserve them.

The Shift I Had to Make

At Icon, I thought I was doing strategic work. But it was all working IN the business because everything required me.

I was in every client meeting, especially the "strategic" ones. I made every hiring decision because I was the bottleneck. I solved every complex problem because nobody else had authority. I was the person everyone waited for because I'd trained them to wait.

I thought I was working ON the business because the work felt important and strategic.

But the test was clear: if I disappeared for a week, Icon would struggle. Because *I WAS* the system.

What I came to realise was that working ON the business meant:

• Building Role Agreements so people knew what they owned, rather than
me owning everything.

• Creating the Oversight Loop so drift got caught systematically,

rather than me catching it.

• Developing my leadership team to make decisions, rather than me

making all decisions.

• Documenting processes so knowledge lived in the system, not in my

head.

• Protecting time to think strategically, not filling every gap

reactively.

This work felt less urgent. Less heroic. Less "needed."

But it was the only work that built the business instead of building my indispensability.

How to Know Which One You're Doing

This expands on the simple test I shared with you earlier. After you finish anything important, ask yourself three questions:

1\. If this situation happens again, who will handle it?

If the answer is "me" → Working IN

If the answer is "the person who owns this" or "the system" → Working ON

2\. Did the business get less dependent on me because of what I just did?

If no → Working IN

If yes → Working ON

3\. What did I build?

If you built an outcome → Working IN

If you built capacity, clarity, or process → Working ON

The Oversight Definition

Here's how I think about it now:

Working IN the business = Filling every gap. You're the person everything needs. The system is you.

Working ON the business = Building the architecture. You're designing systems that function without needing you to be the glue. The system is the system.

Why Most Founders Stay IN

Because working IN FEELS like working ON when you're doing important work.

Strategic client meeting? Feels like ON. But if you're the one maintaining the relationship, you're working IN.

Big hiring decision? Feels like ON. But if you're the bottleneck, you're working IN.

Complex problem-solving? Feels like ON. But if you're the one solving it rather than empowering others to solve it, you're working IN.

The work can be strategic, important, high-level, and still be working IN the business if it builds YOU instead of building SYSTEMS.

The Shift Oversight Creates

Oversight gives you the framework to work ON the business:

• Role Agreements define who owns what, so you're not the default
owner of everything.

• The Oversight Loop catches drift systematically, so you're not the
one catching everything.

• The Drift Map reveals where you're the glue, so you can build
architecture instead.

• External Calibration shows you what you can't see, because you can't
diagnose yourself while being the system.

This is how you move from working IN to working ON – not by doing different types of work, but by doing work that builds the system instead of building your indispensability. And these are the elements I'll share with you throughout the rest of this book.

A Necessary Season

Let me acknowledge something important: being the glue has a necessary season.

In the early years, your personal involvement IS the business. Your hustle, your standards, your relationships: they are the product. The founder who tries to build architecture before they have something worth architecting is solving the wrong problem.

The danger is not being the glue at the start. The danger is staying the glue past the point where it serves the business.

This book is not for founders in year one. It is for founders in year five, year ten, year twenty, who have built something real but are still operating like they are in survival mode. It is for founders who have outgrown the founder-as-glue model but have not yet built what replaces it.

If that is you, read on.

The Deeper Problem

If you're reading this book, you've probably already tried systems. Accountability frameworks. Delegation strategies. Maybe they worked for a while. Maybe they didn't stick. That's because most founders aren't held back by lack of systems. They're held back because the psychological cost of letting go feels too high.

You know you need to delegate, but the thought makes your chest tighten.

You know you need systems, but every time you try to step back, something breaks and you have to step back in.

You know you're working unsustainable hours, but you can't see how to get everything done without everything falling apart.

This isn't a systems problem. This is an architecture problem that must address both structure and psyche at the same time.

Oversight does that. It helps you build the outer structure – Role Agreements, visibility systems, accountability loops – all while navigating the inner obstacles: the Zero Principle, the Hero's Death, identity separation.

The external systems can only hold when the internal work is done. I'll cover both the external systems and the internal work with you in the coming chapters.

The External Vantage Point

What I realised was this: Oversight is objective, and I was not.

I could only see my business through my own lens. But the reality was that there were fifty people employed, external consultants, and hundreds of clients. Each of these people had their own view of my business. Yet I could only see mine.

Oversight allowed me to stop looking at the systems and see the glue holding the systems together. That was me. That glue was the heart of the leader. It represented the values, the beliefs, the identity, the legacy of the leader.

Oversight gave me the ability to see the business from a different vantage point. The unseen framework that keeps everything together when pressure hits. The system that connects values to behaviours, strategy to results, and leaders to renewal.

It was the thing I didn't know I needed until everything fell apart.

And once I saw it, I couldn't unsee it.

This is where the shift begins for every founder. It's the moment you realise that control is a burden, but Oversight is freedom.

The CEO Role Agreement Redefined

Before I talk about what systems you need to put in place for your team, I need to talk about your role as CEO. For decades, we've been operating with a broken understanding of the CEO's role.

We've inherited job descriptions from the industrial age, from command-and-control companies, from a world where the CEO was the smartest person in the room making all the decisions.

That paradigm is dead. And it should be.

The role of the CEO in an Oversight structure is transformed. It requires you to let go of the hero role and step into something far more powerful: Architect and chief coach.

This isn't less important work. This is more important work. But it requires a complete reimagination of what you do.

The Prison You've Been Living In

In the glue model, your role was everything.

You made all the important decisions. You were the main client interface. You reviewed all major work. You solved all escalated problems. You were available 24/7. You knew everything happening in the business. You were the final quality control. You drove all the sales activity. You maintained all the important relationships. You embodied the culture through personal heroics.

The result you owned? Everything.

How was success measured? By how much you could take without breaking.

That's not a Role Agreement. That's a prison sentence.

And if you're being honest, you already know exactly what I'm talking about. The weight of being the person who holds it all together. The burnout of being everyone's solution. The desperation of wondering when it's your turn to breathe.

What Leadership Actually Becomes

In the Oversight architecture, your role changes completely.

Your key result isn't completing the work. It's creating and sustaining the architecture, the system by which work gets done without you in the middle of it.

This means:

• You create the structures of Oversight instead of being in the middle of every decision.

• You build leaders who develop other leaders instead of followers who

only do what you tell them.

• You hold the vision for the long-term while the short-term gets

handled by your team.

• You preserve and protect the culture through structure, not through

your physical presence.

• You remove the things that prevent the architecture from working –

the bottlenecks, the confusion, the gaps in clarity – but you don't

solve every problem.

• You make only the decisions that absolutely require your

involvement, and that number decreases over time.

• You develop the people who own outcomes to higher levels of

competency. That means asking instead of telling. Challenging

instead of solving.

• You model what the architecture demands. If you say boundaries

matter and you answer emails at midnight, you're teaching your team

that boundaries don't matter. You're teaching them the opposite of

what you're saying.

This is a paradigm shift. From doing to designing. From controlling to coaching. From knowing everything to ensuring other people know, if not everything, enough. From solving problems to developing problem-solvers. From being the hero to building heroes.

This is the CEO as Architect. Your job is to build the system that builds the business.

How You Know It's Working

Success gets measured differently in this model. The business runs well without your daily involvement.

Your leadership team makes decisions independently, which means about ninety percent of decisions happen without your input. Not because you've abandoned them, but because they have the clarity, authority, and capability to decide.

The culture sustains itself through systems, not through your personal charisma.

Your revenue and profits are up while your operational hours are down. Not because you're not working hard, because the architecture is holding.

Successor capability is being built into the organisation, not concentrated in individuals.

Seventy percent or more of your time is spent on architectural work, thinking three years ahead, instead of firefighting.

Your team's work is developing other leaders, not getting tasks done.

And perhaps most importantly: the business could function without you for an extended period. Not because you're not valuable, but because your value has been embedded into the system instead of locked into your personal involvement.

When you reach this point, you realise you've actually become more essential by being less involved. The architecture you've built is your greatest contribution, instead of your heroics stealing the show.

The Doubt That Undermines Everything

But what keeps most founders from getting there?

The question that sits in the back of your mind, especially at 3AM when you can't sleep:

"What if my team can't handle it without me?"

That doubt is the quiet saboteur. It undermines every attempt at delegation, every move toward stepping back, every opportunity to build something sustainable.

And the doubt feels rational. You've spent years rescuing your team from mistakes, filling gaps when things got tough, being the one who made sure nothing slipped through the cracks. Of course they need you. Look at what happens when you're not there.

But here's the thing: your team isn't incompetent. They've been trained in co-dependency.

You've done it for years. You taught them to wait for you. When they came to you with a problem, you solved it. When they hesitated on a decision, you made it. When something started to falter, you fixed it before it became their problem to solve. You did it out of care, out of wanting to help. And you taught them that their judgement wasn't needed because yours was available.

This is the rescuer trap. You doubt their capability based on behaviour you created. You've never given them the chance to prove to you that they are more than capable.

The falter they have that makes you wonder if they can handle it? That's not proof they can't. That's them learning to stand. It's what happens when people who've been trained to depend on you must learn to walk on their own.

And yes, they'll stumble. There will be mistakes. Decisions will be made differently than you would have made them.

But that's not failure. That's growth.

How Trust Gets Built

Trust isn't hope. Trust is architecture.

When you're building your trust architecture, you shift from assigning tasks to establishing Role Agreements. You give your team what they need: clear outcomes, ownership of those outcomes, ways to measure success, authority to make decisions, and support when they need it. You hold them accountable for results, not for doing things your way.

The withdrawal period will be uncomfortable. You'll see them struggle with decisions that seem obvious to you. You'll bite your tongue as they make choices you wouldn't have made. You'll feel the urge to step in and rescue.

Don't.

Create safe space for small failures in low-risk situations. Let them learn from experience, not from your intervention.

Use accountability loops for reflection without blame. Ask, "What did we learn?" instead of "Why did you do that?"

If they're struggling, resist the temptation to solve the problem. Ask: "What do you need to own this completely?" and give them what they ask you for.

In one-on-ones, shift the conversation from "what you did this week" to "what you're learning, where you're stuck, and what support you need."

Watch what happens when you start treating them like capable people who are learning instead of children who need constant supervision.

The trust builds. Decision by decision. Then a whole month goes by where you realise you weren't in the middle of something and it turned out fine. Then a quarter. Then you take a full week off and come back to find they didn't just survive, they pushed things forward.

In my story, I was terrified the team couldn't handle things without me. That the business would fail. That clients would leave. That quality would suffer. That it would all fall apart.

But when I let go, built the architecture and learned to trust, my team didn't just hold. They soared.

I realised that what had held us back was my doubt, not their capability.

They were ready. I'd just never given them the opportunity to show it.

If this question is stopping you, if the fear that they can't handle it keeps you stuck as the glue, ask yourself this:

"What if they can, and they're waiting for you to believe it?"

The architecture doesn't structure the work. It enables the people.

Trust it to develop them too.

Now that we've named the weight you're carrying, let's build the architecture that lifts it.

PART II

FRAMEWORKS IN PRACTICE

How Oversight Becomes the Architecture That Holds

Before we dive into building this architecture piece by piece, you need to see the complete picture of what we're building together.

I made this mistake at Icon. I'd grab frameworks from consultants, implement pieces of systems, and try tactics that worked for other businesses. Role Agreements here. Accountability loops there. All of it good on paper.

None of it held.

Why? Because I was building disconnected pieces, not architecture. And disconnected pieces collapse under pressure no matter how well-designed each individual component is.

What follows is the complete architecture that transforms businesses from founder-dependent operations into organisations that function without you being the glue. This is not theory – it's the actual framework I now build with every founder I work with.

The Foundation: The Architecture Triangle

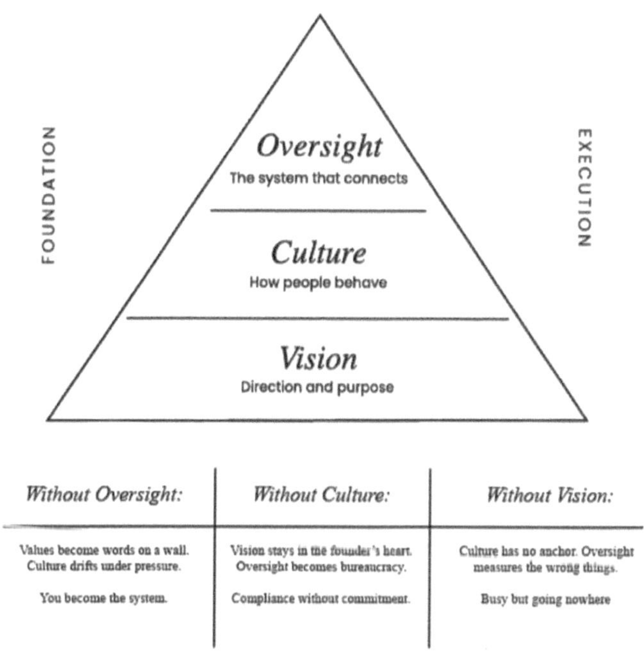

Figure 1: The Architecture Triangle

Everything starts here. Three layers that have to work together.

At the base, you've got **Values**. Why does any of this matter? What do you stand for? What won't you compromise on even when it gets hard?

Then **Culture** in the middle. How do values translate into what happens every day – the way your team treats each other, what behaviours actually get reinforced, what it feels like to work there?

And at the top, **Oversight**. How do you know what's working? How do you catch drift before it turns into a five-alarm fire? How do you maintain standards without being in the middle of everything?

For years at Icon, I had the first two layers beautifully built. Our values – Love and Service – were real. Our culture was alive. People genuinely cared about each other and the work.

But without Oversight holding the top, the triangle couldn't keep its shape when pressure hit.

COVID made that visible. I couldn't be physically present. The team worked remotely. Decisions had to happen without me in the room. And suddenly everything I thought was solid started faltering.

Values drifted; not because people stopped caring, but because there was no system to translate values into consistent behaviour when I wasn't there modelling them.

Culture weakened; not because relationships disappeared, but because culture built on my proximity couldn't survive distance without structure.

I became the missing structure. That led to seventy-hour weeks on Zoom trying to be the connective tissue the architecture should have provided.

That's when I saw it clearly: Values without Culture = words on a wall. Culture without Oversight = momentum that can't survive pressure. Oversight without Values = bureaucracy nobody wants to follow.

You need all three. And your job as the leader is to build all three, not to personally be all three.

What Oversight Actually Does

Oversight is not micromanagement. It's not control. It's not watching over shoulders or creating bureaucratic approval processes.

Oversight is the system that holds the system.

In most businesses, once you delegate a task, the person knows what to do but not what they own. When you create Oversight architecture, they know the outcome they're responsible for, how success gets measured, what authority they have, and how drift gets caught early before it becomes crisis.

Oversight turns values into actual behaviours instead of poster slogans. Values say "we care about quality". But Oversight defines what quality means, how it's measured, who owns it, and what happens when it slips.

It makes culture consistent instead of dependent on you remembering to reinforce it. The weekly loops, the one-on-ones, the check-ins – all of that becomes systematic instead of something that only happens when you're paying attention.

And it shifts leadership from reactive firefighting to intentional building. Without Oversight, you're just responding to whatever breaks loudest. With Oversight, you see drift before it becomes fire. You catch misalignment before it becomes conflict. You build capability instead of constantly rescuing.

Oversight is built on four essential pillars.

The Four Pillars of Oversight

1. External Collaboration	2. Outcome Ownership	3. The Human Architech	4. The Oversight Loop
You can't see your own drift. This pillar is about finding someone outside the emotional fog who can hold the mirror steady and tell you the truth you need to hear.	People don't own tasks; They own results. Role agreements make crystal clear what someone owns, how success gets measured, and what authority they have.	Ownaship only becomes sustainable when it connects to the actual human: their personal values, professiooonal growth, outcomes, and cultural behaviours.	Systems need rythm or they die. The operating heartbeat: Clarity→ Alignment → Accountability → Renewal → Clarity.

Without External Collaboration:	*Without Outcome Ownership:*	*Without the Human Architech:*	*Without The Oversight Loop:*
You measure what you think matters while being blind to what's actually breaking. Beautiful dashboards tracking the wrong things.	You see the problems clearly but no one owns the solutions. Nothing changes because accountability lives nowhere.	People hit the metrics for a while, then burn out. Ownership disconnected from meaning doesn't sustain.	People know what they own and why it matters, but there's no cadence catching drift. By the time you notice, it's already a crisis.
Confident but lost.	Awareness without action.	Performance without purpose.	Good intentions, no rhthym

These are the load-bearing walls. Pull one out and the whole thing becomes unstable.

PILLAR ONE: External Calibration

You can't see your own drift. No founder can. You're too close, too invested, too tangled in the daily operations. This pillar is about finding someone outside the emotional fog – someone who can hold the mirror steady when you're shaking and tell you the truth you need to hear, not the truth you want to hear.

PILLAR TWO: Outcome Ownership

People don't own tasks; they own results. That shift – from "I did the activities" to "I delivered the outcome" – changes everything. This happens through Role Agreements that make it crystal clear what someone owns, how success gets measured, and what authority they have to make it happen.

PILLAR THREE: The Human Architecture

Here's where most frameworks fail. They treat people like components in a machine. But ownership only becomes sustainable when it connects to the actual human doing the owning. By which I mean their personal values, their professional growth, the outcomes they're responsible for, and the cultural behaviours that make all of it work. Strip away that human layer and people just burn out hitting metrics.

PILLAR FOUR: The Oversight Loop

Systems need rhythm or they die. This pillar creates the operating heartbeat: Clarity → Alignment → Accountability → Renewal → Clarity. It's what catches drift before it becomes a crisis. It's what makes everything else sustainable instead of just another initiative that fades after three months.

How the Pillars Work Together

You can't cherry-pick. That's what I tried to do at Icon and it didn't work.

You can have External Calibration – someone telling you what's broken – but if no one owns the solutions, nothing changes. You see the problems more clearly while still being powerless to fix them.

You can give people Outcome Ownership – clear results to deliver – but if that ownership doesn't connect to who they are as humans, they'll hit the metrics for a while and then burn out. I've watched it happen.

The Human Architecture piece is essential, but without the Oversight Loop creating rhythm, the system wavers. People know what they own and why it matters, but there's no cadence catching drift early. So by the time you notice something's wrong, it's already a crisis.

And the Oversight Loop without External Calibration? You're measuring what you think matters while being completely blind to what's actually breaking. You've got beautiful dashboards tracking the wrong things.

Each of the four pillars reinforce each other. They protect each other. And when all four are built and working together, that's when the business starts operating without you being the glue holding every piece in place.

Now you've seen the complete architecture, let's build it.

CHAPTER 4

Crossing the Threshold: When Oversight Begins

It was 2015 when I first admitted I needed help.

Icon was growing. Revenue was strong. The team was expanding. On paper, everything looked right. But I was working seventy-hour weeks and couldn't see a way out. Every decision still flowed through me. Every problem landed on my desk.

So I did something I'd never done before: I brought in a consultant.

The Consultant Who Changed Everything

He spent not weeks, but months with us. Observing meetings. Talking to the team. Reviewing how decisions got made, how work flowed, where things stalled. I expected him to find problems with our systems. Our processes. Our tools.

Instead, he found me.

One afternoon, he sat across from me in my office and said: "Your problem isn't systems. You have systems. Your problem is that none of your people own anything."

I pushed back. "Of course they do. They have roles. Responsibilities."

"Tasks," he interrupted. "They have tasks. But who owns client retention? Who owns quality standards? Who owns capacity management? Who owns culture?"

The silence was uncomfortable.

"You do," he said quietly. "You own all of it. And your team knows it. So they wait for you."

He introduced me to something he called Role Agreements. These were not job descriptions, but outcome ownership. Clear definitions of what each person was responsible for achieving, how success would be measured, and what authority they had to make decisions.

Over the following months, we built them together. Progressively. Carefully. Each role was redefined around outcomes rather than activities. Each person was given real authority to deliver results.

And it worked.

Decisions started happening without me. Problems got solved at the source. The team stepped up in ways I hadn't seen before. I started reclaiming hours from my week.

I thought I'd found the answer.

What COVID Revealed

For five years, the Role Agreements held. The business grew. The team strengthened. I genuinely believed we'd cracked it.

Then COVID hit.

Within weeks, everything I thought was solid started to waver. Not because the Role Agreements failed – operationally, they still worked. People knew what they owned. Decisions still got made.

But something deeper was fracturing.

Communication scattered. Alignment drifted. The culture I'd built on proximity, on being in the room – reading faces, catching small signals – couldn't survive distance. People were isolated, anxious, and disconnected from meaning.

And I found myself working harder than ever. Seventy hours became eighty. I was on every Zoom call, in every decision, trying to be the connective tissue that held everyone together.

That's when I realised: Role Agreements had given people ownership of outcomes. But I'd never built the architecture that would catch drift before it became crisis. I'd never created the systems that would maintain alignment without me being in the middle of everything.

The consultant had solved one problem. But COVID exposed a deeper one.

Role Agreements were necessary. But they weren't sufficient.

The Question That Changed Everything

As the pandemic dragged on, I kept returning to something the consultant had said on his last day.

He'd paused at the door, turned back, and said: "Maybe you're not fit to go from founder to managing a bigger business."

At the time, I was angry. Who was he to question me? I'd built Icon from nothing. I'd survived brutal years in a competitive industry.

But underneath the anger was fear. What if he was right?

What if the skills that made me a successful founder – the ability to hustle, solve problems, be in everything – were exactly the skills preventing me from building something that could outlast my personal involvement?

COVID forced me to sit with that question.

And I realised: he wasn't questioning my competence. He was questioning my identity.

Was I a founder who needed to be indispensable? Or was I a leader who could build something bigger than my personal involvement?

Building What Was Missing

From 2020 to 2023, I worked to answer that question by building what the Role Agreements had been missing.

Not just Outcome Ownership, but the Human Architecture that makes ownership sustainable. Not just clarity about who owns what, but the Oversight systems that catch drift before it becomes a crisis. Not just delegation, but the rhythm of alignment and accountability that keeps everything connected.

The full architecture. Values at the base. Culture in the middle. Oversight at the top.

Slowly, something shifted.

The team started making decisions without me, not because I'd taught them what to decide, but because they knew what they owned and had the systems to stay aligned.

Problems got caught earlier. Not because I was more vigilant, but because the architecture surfaced drift before it became a fire.

I started working fewer hours. Not because the business was smaller, but because the architecture was holding.

By mid-2023, when I made the decision to sell Icon, it wasn't because the business was failing. It was because the business was finally functioning without me. And the reason I knew that was because the Oversight architecture gave me the vantage point to see it.

The Real Answer

Looking back, I understand what that consultant was really asking in 2015.

He wasn't questioning whether I had the ability to manage a bigger business. He was asking whether I had the willingness to stop being the person who managed everything. He was asking, though I didn't understand it then, whether I was capable of moving from founder to Architect.

The Role Agreements he introduced were the first step. But it took COVID to show me they weren't enough. It took three years of building to complete the architecture.

And once I crossed that threshold, once I proved to myself that I could build something that held without me being the glue, I realised something profound.

I'd spent twenty years helping founders grow their revenue while watching them struggle with the exact same question that consultant had asked me.

They weren't unfit to manage bigger businesses. They lacked the architecture that would allow their capability to scale beyond their personal involvement.

They needed Oversight.

They needed someone who'd lived through that question and built the architecture that answered it.

That's when Two Icons was born.

Where the Shift Begins

This realisation is where the shift begins for every founder.

Not when you have all the answers. Not when you've built perfect systems. Not when your team is fully capable and nothing ever wavers.

The shift begins when you realise that drift isn't a sign of failure. It's a sign that the architecture is missing.

And architecture can be built.

You don't need to work harder. You don't need better people. You don't need more willpower.

You need the complete architecture: External Calibration to see what you can't see, Outcome Ownership to transfer real responsibility, Human Architecture to make ownership sustainable, and the Oversight Loop to catch drift before it becomes a crisis.

The gap between what you intend and what happens? That's not a character flaw. It's evidence that you're trying to build a sustainable business with incomplete architecture.

Once you see that, everything changes.

Because you can build what's missing.

You can cross the threshold from being the glue to being the Architect.

And that's exactly where we're going next.

CHAPTER 5

The External Vantage Point: The Mirror You Won't Let Anyone Hold

For most of Icon's twenty years, I had external advisors.

An accountant who reviewed our financials quarterly. A lawyer who kept us compliant with employment law and contracts. A business coach I'd meet with twice a year. Industry peers I'd grab coffee with to talk through challenges.

They were competent. Well-meaning. Experienced.

And they were completely useless at giving me what I actually needed.

Not because they lacked expertise. But because I hadn't given them permission to see what I was protecting.

The Boardroom Where No One Could See

I remember sitting in a boardroom in 2019, surrounded by these advisors. Icon was at its peak – major projects, strong revenue, growing team. On paper, everything looked good.

We were reviewing the quarter. The accountant walked through the numbers. All solid. The coach asked about my strategic priorities. I shared them confidently. The peers nodded, offered encouragement, suggested a few tactical tweaks.

The meeting ended. Everyone felt good about Icon's trajectory.

And I walked out feeling completely alone.

Because none of them could see what I saw. Or so I believed.

The truth was harder to acknowledge: I hadn't given anyone permission to see what I saw.

Icon was my creation. My identity. My proof that I mattered. My story of survival and success after twenty years of building.

As a result, I unconsciously protected it from scrutiny.

I didn't want anyone to tell me the things I already felt in the quiet hours at 3AM:

That I was carrying too much.

That my judgement was clouded by exhaustion.

That my identity was tangled in the business.

That my culture was wobbling under pressure.

That my system wouldn't hold without me.

That I was the bottleneck.

So I curated what my advisors could see.

I shared the metrics but not the weight. The strategy but not the fear. The wins but not the 3AM panic. The growth numbers but not the personal cost.

And they responded to what I showed them: congratulations on the growth, here are some tactical suggestions, keep doing what you're doing.

External validation, not External Calibration.

Why External Advisors Fail

Most founders have external advisors. Accountants. Lawyers. Coaches. Consultants. Boards. Peer groups. But most of these relationships fail to provide what Oversight requires: genuine External Calibration.

Here's why: they're designed to keep you safe, not keep you aligned.

An accountant ensures your financials are compliant. A lawyer ensures your contracts protect you. A compliance advisor ensures you meet regulatory requirements. These are important. But they're not calibration.

Calibration requires someone who can see the gap between your intention and your reality. Between what you think is happening and what's really happening. Between the architecture you believe exists and the glue you're actually being.

My external advisors at Icon ensured we were compliant. But they didn't challenge my vantage point. They didn't see the weight I was carrying alone.

Because I didn't let them.

The Lens You Don't Provide

External advisors can only see what you give them a lens to see.

If you show them metrics, they'll comment on metrics. If you show them strategy, they'll comment on strategy. If you show them the curated version of your business, they'll respond to that version.

But if you don't give them the lens to see the architecture, or lack of it, they can't calibrate you to it.

At Icon, I never gave my advisors a framework for looking at the business beyond financials and operations.

I never asked: "Am I the glue? Where is ownership unclear? Where am I compensating for missing architecture with my personal involvement?" I never invited them to challenge whether my proximity was strength or weakness. I never gave them permission to question whether my indispensability was value or fragility.

So they didn't.

And I stayed trapped inside my own perspective, believing I was alone in seeing what I saw, when the truth was: I was alone because I'd made sure no one else could see it.

What External Calibration Actually Requires

This is where we come to the first pillar of Oversight: External Calibration. It comes first because without an outside perspective, you can't see where the other pillars need to be built.

No leader can see their own drift. We're too close. Too emotionally invested. Too tangled in our identity with the business.

Oversight requires a vantage point outside the founder's perspective.

But the hard part is this: it's not enough to have external people. You need external people with the right lens. And you need to give them permission to use it.

True External Calibration is not about checking boxes or reviewing dashboards. It's about holding the mirror steady when the leader is shaking. It requires someone outside the system who can see what you can't, or won't, see yourself.

It requires someone who will say:

"You're too close to see this clearly."

"You're drifting."

"You're carrying weight the business should be carrying."

"Your identity is tangled here, and it's clouding your judgement."

And it requires you to be willing to hear it.

The Voice I Didn't Have

For most of Icon's journey, I didn't have this voice.

Not because it wasn't available. But because I didn't create the conditions for it.

I kept my advisors at arm's length emotionally. I shared data but not struggle. Progress but not panic. Wins but not weight.

I asked for advice on tactics but never on whether I was the problem. I wanted external validation that I was doing well, not External Calibration that I was drifting. So that's what I got.

My advisors would leave meetings thinking Icon was in great shape. And I'd leave feeling more alone than when I walked in. Because no one could see what I was protecting. And I couldn't see that I was the one preventing them from seeing it.

The Mirror and the Maze

Without External Calibration, the leader becomes trapped inside their own maze. You can't see the maze when you're inside it. You can only see the walls directly in front of you, the turns you're navigating, and the dead ends you're trying to avoid.

But someone standing above the maze, someone outside your perspective, outside your identity, outside the emotional fog, can see the whole pattern. They can see where you're going in circles. They can see the exit you keep walking past. They can see that you're the one building the walls that trap you.

This was what I needed at Icon. Not someone to review my P&L. Not someone to ensure compliance. Not someone to validate my strategy.

I needed someone to stand above my maze and tell me what I couldn't see from inside it. But at the time, I didn't know how to ask for that. Or realise that I even needed it.

What This Looks Like in Practice

I work with a founder now, let's call her Maria, who has an executive coach she meets with monthly.

When she first told me about the coach, I asked: "Does your coach give you external calibration or external validation?"

She looked confused. "What's the difference?"

"Does your coach challenge your perspective, or affirm your decisions?"

Long pause. "Affirm, mostly. She's supportive."

"Does she tell you when you're the problem?"

Another pause. "No. She helps me solve problems with my team."

"Have you given her permission to tell you that you might be the bottleneck?"

"\...No. I haven't."

We restructured her coaching relationship around External Calibration. She gave her coach a new lens: the Oversight framework.

Now, when Maria asks: "How can I get my team to step up?" her coach asks: "Where are you preventing them from stepping up?"

When Maria says: "Here's my strategy," her coach responds: "Where is your identity driving this strategy instead of the business needs?"

When Maria complains: "They're not taking ownership," her coach queries: "What architecture is missing that would allow them to own it?"

The shift was uncomfortable. Maria felt more challenged, less supported.

But three months in, she told me: "I have someone who can see what I can't. And it's exactly what I needed."

That's External Calibration.

The Permission You Must Give

External Calibration doesn't happen automatically just because you have external advisors.

It happens when you:

- Give them the right lens (Oversight framework, not metrics)

- Give them permission (to challenge, not just affirm)
- Give them access (to your actual struggles, not curated wins)
- Give them safety (to tell you hard truths without fear of being fired)

At Icon, I didn't give my advisors any of this. So they gave me what I was asking for: validation that I was doing well. And I stayed trapped inside my own maze, blinded by my own brilliance, carrying weight I couldn't see was mine to release.

Where External Calibration Fits in Oversight

External Calibration is the first pillar because you can't see your own drift from inside your own perspective. You need the outside view before you can build what's inside.

You need both:

External Calibration (the outside lens) to see where the architecture is weak and where you're compensating for it.

AND

The internal pillars (Outcome Ownership, Human Architecture, Oversight Loop) to create the structure that holds without you.

Without External Calibration, you can't see where the architecture is failing, even though you know it is, because you're the one inside the failure.

Without the internal architecture, there's nothing for external eyes to calibrate against.

Both are required.

What I Wish I'd Known

If I could go back to 2019, sitting in that boardroom with my advisors, feeling alone, I would do two things:

First: I'd give them the Oversight lens. I'd ask them to look not at our metrics, but at our architecture. Where ownership was unclear. Where I was the glue. Where drift was hiding.

Second: I'd give them permission to tell me I was the problem. Not the team. Not the market. Not the systems. Me. My identity. My proximity. My unwillingness to let go.

I didn't do either of those things. Because I didn't know I needed to.

But you do. Which means you can.

Where to Go Deeper

External Calibration isn't about hiring more advisors. It's about giving your existing advisors (or new ones) the right lens and permission to use it.

The Oversight framework gives them that lens:

- Are Role Agreements clear? (Chapter 6)
- Is the Oversight Loop catching drift? (Chapter 8)
- Is the founder compensating for missing architecture? (Chapter 10)

For practical tools to support your External Calibration journey, see the Resources section at the end of this book.

But before you reach for external help, ask yourself:

Have I given anyone permission to tell me I'm the problem?

Have I created safety for someone to challenge my perspective?

Am I asking for validation or calibration?

Because external advisors can only give you what you're willing to receive. And if you're protecting your identity like I was, no amount of external expertise will penetrate the walls you've built.

The mirror only works if you're willing to look in it.

But External Calibration is only one pillar. The next step is Outcome Ownership, the second pillar, starting with how your team understands what they own.

CHAPTER 6

From Tasks to Ownership: When Role Agreements Meet Reality

Most businesses run on job descriptions: tidy documents written in tidy language that describe tidy tasks. "Manage client relationships. Coordinate project delivery. Conduct team meetings. Report on metrics."

Tasks, tasks, tasks.

And what happens? People do exactly what's written in their job descriptions. Nothing more, nothing less. Not because they lack initiative. Because the system doesn't ask for ownership, it asks for activity.

At Icon, I watched this play out for years. Team members checked every box on their job descriptions while the business drifted. They completed tasks while outcomes slipped. They were busy, productive, compliant. And I was still the one worrying about whether we'd hit our retention target, whether quality was holding, whether clients were happy.

Because nobody owned those outcomes. I did.

The rescue habit isn't rare. Research consistently shows most founders continue intervening in day-to-day decisions long after they've delegated. Teams under high-intervention leaders show markedly lower ownership and higher turnover intent. And nearly half of all founders admit that fear of team failure keeps them from stepping back, even when they know it's limiting growth.

I was that founder. Delegating tasks while hoarding outcomes.

The Role Agreement Breakthrough

The consultant who arrived in 2015 introduced me to something called Role Agreements, as I shared in Chapter 4.

It felt like the answer I'd been searching for.

Instead of job descriptions listing tasks, Role Agreements defined ownership. They answered three questions:

1. What outcome do you own?

2. How is success measured?

3. What authority do you have to decide?

Clear outcomes. Measurable success. Explicit authority.

We implemented them with my leadership team.

My Head of Client Services owned client retention and satisfaction, measured by a ninety-five percent retention rate, with full authority over client relationships.

My Business Development Manager owned new client acquisition, measured by qualified leads and conversion rates.

My Finance Director owned cash flow and margin, with authority over payment terms and pricing strategy.

And it worked. Genuinely worked.

Decisions that used to flow through me started getting made by the people who owned the outcomes. The leadership team stepped up. The architecture started to take shape.

For the first time in years, I felt like I might be able to step back without everything collapsing.

The Cracks COVID Uncovered

As I shared earlier, for five years, the Role Agreements held. The business grew. The team strengthened. Then COVID hit. And I discovered something I hadn't expected.

My Head of Client Services, one of the most capable people I'd ever worked with, sat across from me in her quarterly review. She was hitting ninety-four percent on a ninety-five percent retention target.

On paper, everything was working.

But as she walked me through the numbers, something felt off. A flatness in her voice. A fatigue that didn't match the results.

"How are you feeling about the role?" I asked.

She hesitated.

"Honestly? Depleted."

"I'm hitting the metrics," she continued. "But I'm working more hours than ever. I wake up at 3AM worrying about the two clients who might churn. I haven't taken a real day off in months because I'm scared something will slip."

She was burning out in plain sight, while succeeding by every measure I'd given her.

The timing wasn't coincidental.

Before the pandemic, we could pretend work and life were separate containers. People showed up, did their jobs, went home. The professional mask held.

COVID shattered that illusion.

Suddenly we were on video calls looking into people's living rooms. Kids wandered through meetings. The carefully maintained boundary between "work self" and "whole self" collapsed, and it's never coming back.

But something deeper shifted too. People started asking questions they'd been too busy to ask before. Questions about meaning. About whether the life they were building fitted the person they wanted to be.

The pandemic didn't create these questions. It gave people the space, and the mortality awareness, to ask them.

And when they came back to work, they brought those questions with them.

The Missing Layer

The Role Agreement I'd given my Head of Client Services was built for the "work version" of a person. It defined what she owned professionally. It measured success by business outcomes. It gave her authority within her functional domain.

But it had nothing to say about who she was outside that domain. Nothing about what mattered to her as a whole human being. Nothing about whether delivering these outcomes was building a life she actually wanted, or slowly dismantling it.

We had Role Agreements. We had Outcome Ownership. We had metrics and authority.

But we didn't have architecture for the whole person.

She knew what she owned. She knew how success was measured.

But she didn't know why it mattered to her personally. She didn't see how this outcome connected to what she cared about in life. And she was burning out trying to prove she could handle the ownership I'd given her, while the rest of her life paid the price.

I'd given her a framework built for the old world. And the old world was gone.

The Human Architecture

	KEY QUESTION	
CULTURAL Values in action. *What behaviours protect the achitecture?*	How do values show up in this role?	
ORGANISATIONAL Business outcomes *What does this role own? What metrics define success?*	What outcomes do they own?	
PROFESSIONAL Career growth *What skills are they building? Where are they heading?*	How does this role serve their growth?	COMPLETE ROLE AGREEMENT — THE PACT
PERSONAL Life outside work *What booundaries matter? What coommitments exist outside?*	What does their life require?	

Without Human Architecture:	*With Human Architecture:*
People burn out hitting metrics. Role Agreements become task lists.	Ownership connects to the whole person. Sustainable performance becomes possible.

Figure 2: Human Architecture – The Four Layers of The Pact

This is the third pillar of Oversight, and it's the one most founders skip because it feels "soft."

It's not soft. It's structural.

Human Architecture is the integration of the second pillar, Outcome Ownership, with who the person actually is. These second and third pillars of Oversight are inextricably linked. One won't succeed without the other. The third pillar of Human Architecture builds on four layers:

The Personal Layer. What does this person care about outside work? Time with family? Financial security? Creative expression? Health? These aren't separate from their role: they're the foundation of why they show up.

The Professional Layer. What mastery are they building? What skills matter to them? Where do they want to grow? People want to become something through their work, not just produce something.

The Organisational Layer. What outcome do they own? How is success measured? What authority do they have? This is the Role Agreement itself, which is necessary, but no longer sufficient in isolation.

The Cultural Layer. What behaviours protect the architecture? How do values translate into how this ownership looks? Culture is what keeps people when salary isn't the deciding factor.

When all four layers align, ownership becomes sustainable. Without them, it becomes a more sophisticated way to burn people out.

Redesigning the Architecture

I went back to my Head of Client Services.

"What do you care about most outside work?" I asked.

She looked surprised. In all our years working together, I'd never asked her that.

"Being present for my kids," she said. "They're 11 and 13 now. I feel like I'm missing everything."

"How many hours are you working to hit your retention targets?"

"Fifty to sixty a week. Sometimes weekends."

The Role Agreement was working operationally. But it was destroying what she actually valued. The question wasn't whether she could handle the ownership. She clearly could. The question was whether the ownership was worth what it was costing her.

So we redesigned her ownership with all four layers integrated:

Personal: Be home for dinner five nights a week. No weekend work except true emergencies. This wasn't a perk: it was a structural requirement of the role.

Professional: Build team capability that doesn't depend on her hours. Develop two senior account managers who can own sub-outcomes. Her growth path wasn't just "retain more clients"; it was "build a team that can retain clients without burning anyone out."

Organisational: Own client retention and satisfaction, measured by retention rate AND sustainable team capacity. That looked like no one working over 45 hours consistently. The metric itself had to change.

Cultural: Model the boundary-setting and renewal rhythms the whole organisation needed to see. She wasn't just protecting herself. She was demonstrating what sustainable leadership looks like.

After we made those changes, the metrics didn't suffer. They improved. Because the human foundation was in place.

Six months later, she told me: "This is the first time in my career I've felt like I'm doing work that matters in a way that fits who I am."

Her performance didn't just improve: her presence changed. She went from going through the motions to protecting the architecture like it was hers.

Because it finally was.

This wasn't a Role Agreement anymore. A Role Agreement tells someone what they own. This was something different. Something mutual. A commitment between two people: I'll build this architecture around who you actually are, and you'll protect it like it matters. Because it does.

I started calling it The Pact.

The Universal Pattern

Her story isn't unique. It's universal.

Every founder I work with has someone like her. Someone capable, someone delivering, someone quietly wondering whether the trade-offs are worth it. Pre-COVID, those people suffered in silence. Post-COVID, they leave.

The businesses that will thrive aren't the ones with the best Role Agreements. They're the ones that have moved beyond Role Agreements entirely.

Think about the progression most businesses go through:

A **Job Description** tells someone what to do. It lists tasks. It defines activity. And people do exactly what's written, nothing more, nothing less. The business gets compliance.

A **Role Agreement** tells someone what to own. It defines outcomes, metrics, authority. It's a genuine leap forward. The business gets ownership.

The Pact commits both parties to building ownership that honours the whole person. It integrates what someone owns with who they are, where they're going, and what they value. The business gets transformation.

Each stage is a deeper relationship between founder and team member. Each asks more of both parties. A Job Description is handed down. A Role Agreement is negotiated. A Pact is built together.

A note on language: Throughout this book, I use "Role Agreement" as the structural tool – the document that defines what someone owns, how success is measured, and what authority they have. When that Role Agreement incorporates all four layers of Human Architecture – personal, professional, organisational, and cultural – it becomes The Pact. You'll see both terms in the chapters ahead. Think of Role Agreements as the architecture, and The Pact as the architecture with a soul.

Role Agreements without Human Architecture create sophisticated depletion. People know exactly what's expected of them, they deliver on it, and they slowly hollow out in the process.

The Pact asks a different set of questions. Four questions that, when aligned, change everything:

1. What do I actually care about as a human, and how does this outcome connect to that?

2. Where am I trying to go professionally, and how does this role build me toward that?

3. What result am I responsible for, and what authority do I have to deliver it?

4. What behaviours will keep this sustainable, for me, for the team, for the business?

When those four questions align, people don't just deliver outcomes. They transform. And they stay.

Human Architecture doesn't replace the other pillars. It integrates with them.

External Calibration helps you see when people are drifting, when the outcome they own is disconnecting from who they are. You need that outside voice to catch it before they burn out or walk out.

Outcome Ownership gives people clear results to deliver. But Human Architecture ensures those results connect to who they are and where they're going.

Then the Oversight Loop, which we'll get to next, creates the rhythm that maintains all four layers.

Skip this pillar, skip the human integration, and the whole architecture becomes mechanical. Functional but hollow. And in the post-COVID world, hollow doesn't inspire.

It empties out.

Where to Go Deeper

Role Agreements aren't just documentation. They're the architecture that transfers real ownership from you to your team. But ownership only sticks when it connects to the whole person, not just their job function.

That's why Role Agreements and The Pact work together:

• Role Agreements define what someone owns and how success is measured

• The Pact connects that ownership to who they are: their values,

their growth, their boundaries

Without Role Agreements, people do tasks but don't own outcomes. Without The Pact, people hit metrics but burn out.

If you're seeing these patterns, here's where to look:

• Team waiting for your decisions → Role Agreements lack clear

authority (this chapter).

• High performers burning out → The Pact is missing the renewal layer

(this chapter).

• Drift happening between check-ins → The Oversight Loop needs rhythm

(Chapter 7).

• You're still the glue despite delegation → The Drift Map will show

you where (Chapter 8).

For practical templates including Role Agreement structures and Pact conversation guides, see the Resources section at the end of this book.

But before you reach for the templates, ask yourself:

Have I given my people real ownership, or just more tasks with my fingerprints still on them?

Do I know what my team members actually value, or just what they deliver?

Am I building people who can thrive, or just perform?

Because Role Agreements without The Pact create compliance. And compliance doesn't hold when pressure hits. Only ownership does. And ownership only comes when people feel seen as whole humans, not just functions in your system.

What I Almost Missed

But here's what my Head of Client Services also revealed: I only knew she was burning out because she told me.

Six months of burnout. Six months of 3AM wake-ups. Six months of her life slipping away from her.

And I hadn't seen any of it.

I was relying on proximity and instinct, the same founder radar that had kept me trapped in the middle of everything for twenty years. But proximity doesn't scale. And instinct only catches what's already visible.

What if she hadn't said anything? What if she'd quietly resigned?

I needed architecture that caught drift before it became a breaking point or a resignation letter.

That's where the Oversight Loop comes in.

The Oversight Loop: The Rhythm That Catches Drift

For years at Icon, I led through adrenaline and proximity.

Something would start to slip, and I'd feel it. A client relationship getting tense. A team member disengaging. Quality starting to falter. I'd jump in, fix it, move on.

I thought this was good leadership: staying close, catching problems early, keeping everything aligned. But I was burned out. And the problems kept coming, because I wasn't catching drift early. I was catching it when it had already spread through the system and become visible enough to trigger my alarm bells.

By then, it wasn't early. It was appearing on my radar just before the critical moment.

My Head of Client Services had made this painfully clear. She'd been burning out for six months, and I only knew because she told me. My proximity-based leadership, the thing I'd prided myself on, had completely missed it.

If she hadn't spoken up, I would have lost her. And I would have had no idea why. That's when I realised: I didn't have a system for catching drift. I had me. And I was failing.

Drift doesn't announce itself. It doesn't arrive with a crisis or a blowup or a dramatic moment where everything falls apart.

Drift begins quietly.

It begins when communication becomes slightly less clear. When expectations become slightly less aligned. When decisions take slightly longer. When people hesitate instead of acting. When meetings feel heavier. When energy feels flatter. When the leader starts filling in gaps without realising they're doing it.

Drift is subtle. Drift is slow. Drift is silent.

And drift is dangerous.

By the time I could feel drift at Icon, when something triggered that founder alarm system in my gut, it had already been spreading for weeks, sometimes months.

A client relationship wasn't tense yesterday. It had been deteriorating through small misalignments over the past six weeks. I just didn't have visibility to spot it until the tension became obvious.

A team member wasn't suddenly disengaged. They'd been slowly checking out as clarity eroded and ownership blurred. I just noticed when the withdrawal became undeniable.

Quality wasn't faltering today. Standards had been slipping incrementally as accountability loops weakened. I only saw it when a client complained.

This is the problem with leading through adrenaline and proximity: you don't see drift until it forces you to see it. And by then, you're firefighting, not architecting.

The Oversight Loop

After I sold Icon and started working with other founders, I realised what had been missing: a systematic rhythm that catches drift before it becomes visible.

Not my personal vigilance. Not my founder intuition. Not my exhausting habit of staying close to everything. But an architectural loop that surfaces misalignment early, when it's still small, still correctable, still before it spreads.

The Oversight Loop has four stages that flow into each other continuously:

Clarity → Alignment → Accountability → Renewal

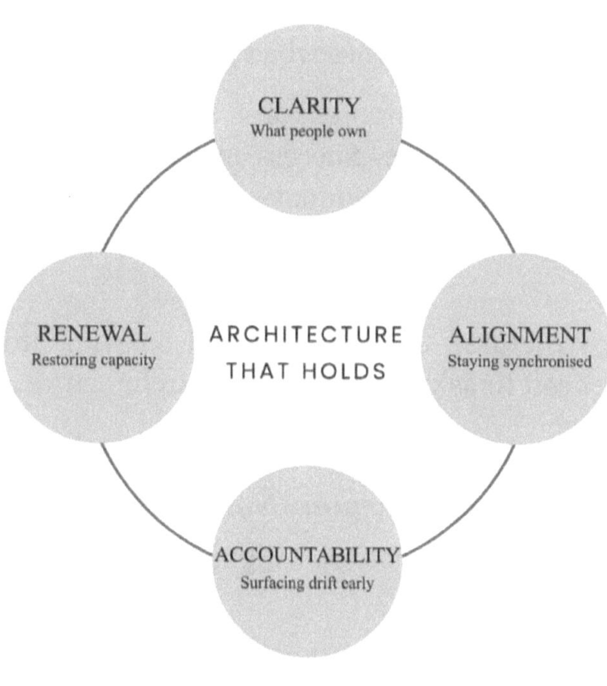

Figure 3: The Oversight Loop

It's not a one-time implementation. It's a continuous rhythm. And it's the heartbeat of the architecture.

Clarity: Where It All Begins

Drift begins when clarity ends.

When people don't know what they own, they wait for you to tell them. When success isn't clearly defined, they guess. When authority boundaries are blurry, they escalate decisions to you instead of making them.

At Icon, we thought we had clarity. Everyone had job descriptions. Everyone knew their responsibilities. Everyone attended the weekly meetings where I communicated priorities.

But clarity isn't about what you've communicated once. It's about what people can reference when you're not in the room.

Real clarity lives in the architecture: Role Agreements that define Outcome Ownership. Success metrics that show what "good" looks like. Authority boundaries that clarify who decides what. Documented processes that answer "how we do this here."

As clarity is structural, it doesn't depend on your proximity. People don't need to ask you because the architecture answers the question.

Alignment: Keeping Everyone Synchronised

Clarity creates the foundation. Alignment keeps everyone synchronised.

This is where most founders fail. They establish clarity once, usually during an offsite or strategic planning session, then assume it holds.

It doesn't.

Clarity decays. Circumstances change. People forget. Priorities shift. New challenges emerge. External pressures appear. Without systematic alignment, clarity drifts back into assumption.

I worked with a founder, David, whose team had weekly meetings. But every week, he'd leave frustrated because people seemed confused about priorities.

When I sat in on a meeting, I saw why. The meeting was him talking at the team, updating them on what he'd been thinking about. There was no space for them to confirm alignment. No opportunity to surface where clarity had started to blur. No mechanism to catch drift.

We restructured the meeting around three questions:

1. What outcome are you owning this week?

2. Where are you unclear or stuck?

3. What decisions do you need clarity on?

Within a month, the drift stopped spreading. It wasn't that David communicated better. It was that the rhythm created space for alignment to be checked and restored.

Accountability: Visible and Blameless

This is where most founders become uncomfortable. Because accountability sounds like pressure. Like policing. Like having to hold people's feet to the fire when they don't deliver.

In a founder-centric business, that's exactly what it is.

But in Oversight architecture, accountability is different. It's not a consequence of failure. It's a natural byproduct of clarity and alignment. When people own clear outcomes, when success is measurably defined, when the loop checks alignment regularly, accountability becomes visible and blameless.

You're not asking: "Why didn't you do what I expected?"

You're observing: "The metric shows we're off track. What's happening?"

The difference is profound.

At Icon, I used to dread accountability conversations. They felt personal. Like I was criticising the person instead of addressing the outcome. That's because I was the one holding accountability. It was my judgement, my standard, my expectation.

When accountability lives in the architecture, when the metrics show drift, when the loop surfaces misalignment, it becomes a shared observation, not a personal criticism.

I watched David's team shift from defensive to curious when accountability moved into the architecture. Instead of "Why are you disappointed in me?" the conversations became "The retention metric dropped three percent, let's figure out what changed."

Renewal: The Structural Requirement

Here's what I got catastrophically wrong at Icon: I thought if I just worked harder, pushed through, sacrificed more, the business would stabilise and I'd eventually get space to rest.

That space never came.

Because success doesn't automatically create space. Only architecture does.

Renewal is the most misunderstood element of the Oversight Loop. In the old model of "Hero Leadership," renewal was a luxury. A reward for surviving the week. Something you'd get to someday when things calmed down.

But in the world of the Architect, renewal is a structural requirement. Because if the leader is the architecture, and the leader breaks, then the system breaks.

By 2023, I was leading on adrenaline. And adrenaline charges high interest rates, collecting on your health, your marriage, your soul.

As you're emotionally spent, you can't see the horizon. You can't think strategically. You can't lead with presence.

You react. And reactive leadership creates drift.

Renewal isn't about taking a vacation when you're already burned out. It's about building rhythms that restore capacity before it's depleted. Weekly protected time to think, not execute. Monthly full days away from operations. Quarterly extended space to reflect and recalibrate. Annually, building in time for true rest that doesn't require recovery from depletion.

When David implemented structural renewal for himself, something unexpected happened. His team stopped escalating everything to him. Not because they suddenly became more capable. But because when he wasn't constantly available, they had to own their decisions. And the architecture supported them in doing it.

Renewal isn't selfish. It's strategic.

Greatness isn't measured by how much you sacrifice. It's measured by what you build that can hold without you.

The Loop in Motion

The Oversight Loop isn't four separate activities. It's a continuous rhythm:

Clarity establishes what people own. Alignment keeps everyone synchronised as circumstances change. Accountability surfaces drift early, cleanly, and without blame. Renewal restores the capacity to lead architecturally instead of reactively.

Then the loop begins again. Clarity is renewed. Alignment is checked. Accountability is maintained. Renewal is protected.

This is how architecture catches drift before it becomes crisis.

Not through your personal vigilance. Not through proximity and adrenaline. But through a systematic rhythm that makes drift visible when it's still small, still correctable, and before it spreads.

When the Business Begins to Breathe

You know the Oversight Loop is working when the business begins to breathe differently.

Less noise. Things seem to be humming a little smoother. There isn't a line of people wanting to discuss things with you at your door. Your team feels settled. It appears as though you have more time.

Outcomes become predictable without your personal involvement. The team stops asking for permission and starts updating you on decisions they've made. Culture reinforces itself through rituals instead of your constant modelling. Drift gets caught in the weekly alignment check, not in the crisis three months later.

There's a profound moment in this reconstruction when you sit back, exhale, and realise: the business is holding without me being the connective tissue.

That's when you've crossed the threshold.

From firefighting to architecting. From adrenaline to rhythm. From being the system to building the system. And that's when you become the leader your business actually needs.

Where to Go Deeper

The Oversight Loop is the operational heartbeat of the architecture. It's what transforms clarity from a one-time effort into a sustained rhythm that catches drift before it becomes a crisis.

I'm not including the full implementation guide here, such as the specific meeting structures, dashboard templates, accountability frameworks, and renewal protocols. That's not what this book is for.

This book is about understanding what's been missing.

When you're ready to implement, practical tools including meeting structures, templates, and assessment guides are available in the Resources section at the end of this book.

But before you reach for the implementation tools, ask yourself:

Am I willing to trust the rhythm more than my proximity?

Can I let the architecture catch drift instead of my exhausting vigilance?

Am I ready to build a business that breathes without my constant intervention?

Because the Loop only works when you're willing to step out of the middle and let it hold. And that requires something deeper than structural change.

It requires psychological transformation.

CHAPTER 8

The Drift Map: Diagnosing Your Own Complicity

In the previous chapter we explored how drift spreads invisibly through your business and how the Oversight Loop catches it early, systematically surfacing misalignment before it becomes a crisis.

But the Oversight Loop alone isn't enough. You also need a Drift Map. These two tools deliver similar outcomes (catching drift early), but focus in different places and therefore serve different but equally important purposes. Think of it this way...

If the Oversight Loop is the business's regular health check, performed by the team together, the Drift Map is the founder's personal x-ray, revealing where you are complicit in the system's drift.

The Oversight Loop is operational. It runs weekly, monthly, quarterly, catching drift through rhythm and visibility. Your team uses it together. It surfaces misalignment in the business.

The Drift Map is personal. It's a periodic, honest assessment of where YOU are allowing drift, or even creating it. You use it alone. It surfaces your own patterns.

The Loop catches drift in the business. The Drift Map catches drift in the founder.

Both are essential. But this chapter is about you.

Because here's what I didn't tell you: drift doesn't happen TO you. You're often unconsciously allowing it. Sometimes even creating it.

This is the leader's reckoning. And the Drift Map is how you diagnose your own complicity.

Why You Allow Drift

When I was carrying Icon, I wore my proximity like a badge of honour. If I wasn't in the weeds, if I wasn't stepping in to save relationships or fix decisions, then what was I even contributing?

I told myself I was being a good leader. Hands-on. Engaged. Available.

But what I was doing was preventing the architecture from holding.

Every time I stepped in to clarify a decision that should have been clear in a Role Agreement, I was allowing drift in clarity.

Every time I modelled a cultural behaviour instead of building it into a systematic ritual, I was allowing drift in culture.

Every time I followed up on an outcome personally instead of letting the Oversight Loop surface it, I was allowing drift in accountability.

Every time I skipped my renewal rhythm because "the business needed me," I was allowing drift in my own capacity.

Drift thrives because the leader unconsciously becomes its ally.

The lie I told myself: "If I don't do it, it won't get done."

The truth I had to face: "If I keep doing it, no one else will learn to."

Drift as Gravity

Here's a simple truth that it took me years to figure out: drift is not failure. Drift is gravity. It's the constant, quiet pull that draws a business away from its design and back toward the individual strength of the leader.

Gravity never stops. The default state of any system is to drift back toward the founder.

Not because the team is incapable. But because you are familiar.

You are the database they've learned to query.

You are the decision-maker they've learned to wait for.

You are the glue they've learned to depend on.

And the uncomfortable truth: your team learned this because you taught them.

When you answered a question they should have been able to answer from the architecture, you reinforced the pattern. When you made a decision someone else owned, you taught them to wait. When you stepped in instead of letting the system hold, you weakened the architecture.

The Drift Map shows you where you're being pulled back into the centre. In many cases, it isn't that the architecture is weak. It's that you're unconsciously allowing yourself to be pulled.

Four Questions That Reveal Everything

I use this with every founder now. Four simple questions. Uncomfortable answers.

They correspond to the four stages of the Oversight Loop: Clarity, Alignment, Accountability, Renewal.

Use them weekly to catch drift early. Monthly to assess patterns. Quarterly to recalibrate the architecture.

Question 1: Where is communication becoming unclear?

Look for this:

Your team is asking you to interpret decisions, rephrase instructions, or clarify direction that should already be defined in the architecture.

You've become the translator between departments.

People come to you asking, "what did they mean by that?" about communications that should be self-evident.

What this signals: Drift in Clarity.

The architecture isn't answering questions. You are.

Role Agreements might exist on paper, but they're not being referenced. Success metrics might be defined, but they're not guiding decisions. Authority boundaries might be documented, but people still escalate to you.

Assess yourself honestly: most founders step in to clarify because it's faster than fixing the architecture. Many secretly enjoy being needed as the interpreter.

I had to face this at Icon. The answer wasn't comfortable.

Question 2: Where is culture beginning to wobble?

This one hit me hardest.

I'd notice the culture felt different when I wasn't in the room. New hires would be confused about "how we do things here" because it only became clear through proximity to me.

I was the cultural enforcer, the one stepping in to model behaviours, reminding people about values in meetings, holding the standard through my personal example.

What this signals: Drift in Alignment.

Culture is living in your personal example instead of in systematic rituals.

At Icon, our values existed. Love and Service were real. But I hadn't translated them into behaviours. The behaviours existed, but I hadn't built them into rituals. The culture depended on my presence to hold its shape.

I was positioning myself as the cultural guardian because it made me feel essential. I avoided building rituals because I thought "the team should just know our values."

But people can't know what isn't systematically reinforced.

Question 3: Where is accountability blurring?

Watch for this pattern:

You are the only one holding people to outcomes and standards.

Accountability lives in your follow-up, not in the architecture.

When something slips, you're the one who notices and addresses it. The team waits for you to catch what falls through the cracks.

What this signals: Drift in Accountability.

The Oversight Loop isn't catching drift. You are.

At Icon, metrics existed. But I was the only one actively monitoring them. Accountability conversations happened, but they were personal and reactive instead of systematic and blameless.

I held accountability personally because it gave me control. I didn't trust that systematic accountability would work without me. And honestly? I was stepping in to "save" people from the consequences of missing their outcomes, which taught them I'd always be there to catch them.

Question 4: Where is your capacity depleting?

This is the one that finally broke me.

By late 2022, I was working harder than ever despite the business appearing stable on paper. I was exhausted. Isolated. I hadn't taken real time off in years. I'm willing to bet this sounds familiar to you.

My renewal rhythms existed on the calendar. But they got cancelled every time "the business needed me."

What this signals: Drift in Renewal.

You're compensating for architectural gaps with personal energy.

The architecture isn't holding the weight, so you are. And it's unsustainable.

I was wearing fatigue as a badge of dedication. Secretly believing that if I wasn't worn down, I wasn't working hard enough. I was avoiding structural renewal because I was terrified the business would waver without my constant presence.

The Drift Map forced me to see it: I wasn't protecting the business by working through my renewal time. I was destroying my capacity to lead it.

The Reckoning

When I first used the Drift Map on myself at Icon in 2022, I wanted to blame the team.

"They're not stepping up."

"They don't take ownership."

"They wait for me to decide everything."

But the Drift Map forced me to ask: *Why?*

And the answer was devastating.

Because I taught them to.

When I answered instead of pointing them to the Role Agreement.

When I modelled culture instead of building it into rituals.

When I followed up personally instead of letting the loop surface it.

When I worked through my renewal time "just this once."

I was the one allowing drift. I was the one preventing the architecture from holding.

This is what makes the Drift Map different from other diagnostic tools. It's not diagnosing drift in the business. It's diagnosing your own complicity in it.

The uncomfortable truth many founders need to face: you are often the reason the architecture isn't holding. Not because you're incompetent. But because you're unconsciously reinforcing the pattern that makes you indispensable.

The Choice Point

Once you see your complicity, the choice becomes clear every time drift surfaces: will you step in again and reinforce the pattern? Or will you name the drift and build the architecture to hold it?

The client relationship gets tense. You can take it over, reinforcing the pattern, or coach the owner through solving it, building capability.

The decision stalls. Do you make the call, or do you clarify the authority boundary so the owner knows they can decide?

The cultural behaviour slips. You can model it yourself again, or build it into a ritual that holds in the team without you.

Your calendar fills with urgency. Do you cancel renewal time, or do you protect it and let the architecture hold?

This is the daily practice of Oversight: choosing the architecture over your proximity.

It's harder. It's slower. It feels riskier.

But it's the only way the system learns to hold without you.

Using the Drift Map

The Drift Map isn't a one-time diagnostic. It's a regular practice.

Weekly: Run through the four questions in ten minutes. Where did drift show up this week? Where did you step in instead of letting the architecture hold? What will you build to prevent that gap next week?

Monthly: Deeper assessment. Review the patterns. Where is drift recurring? Where are you consistently being pulled back to centre? What architectural gap needs to be addressed?

Quarterly: Strategic recalibration. Is the architecture holding? Where is it weak? What needs to be strengthened? Where are you still the glue?

I worked with a founder, let's call him Alex, who fought me on this at first.

"I don't have time for another diagnostic tool," he said. "I'm already drowning."

I told him: "That's exactly why you need it. You're drowning because you keep stepping in instead of building architecture."

He committed to using it weekly for three months.

The first week, he caught himself answering the same question from three different people. So he built a decision framework into the Role Agreement.

Week five, maybe six, he realised he was the only one enforcing response time standards with clients. Then he built it into a team ritual with peer accountability.

A couple of months in, he'd dropped from working fifty-five hours to forty-two hours per week.

Not because the business got smaller. Because he stopped being the glue.

"The strangest part," Alex told me later, "wasn't getting thirteen hours back. It was realising the business didn't miss me. All those years I thought I was essential. Turns out I was just in the way."

The Architect's Posture

Oversight doesn't eliminate drift. It can't. Drift is gravity. It's constant.

But Oversight gives you the vantage point to see drift before it spreads and the architecture to catch it before it becomes an urgent situation.

The Drift Map is how you stand above the maze instead of wandering lost inside it.

When you use it regularly, you stop reacting to drift and start anticipating it. You see the small gap in clarity before it becomes widespread confusion. You catch the signs of an unstable culture before it becomes a crisis of values. You notice the blur in accountability before it becomes missed outcomes. You protect your capacity before you hit exhaustion.

The enemy is not the drift itself. The enemy is the silence that allows drift to spread unnoticed.

With the Drift Map in hand, you are no longer a victim of gravity. You are the Architect, standing above the maze, keeping the system aligned.

Connecting Back: The Human Foundation

Remember in Chapter 6 when Role Agreements evolved into The Pact, that four-layer ownership that honours the whole person?

Here's the other side of that truth: even with that foundation in place, you can still sabotage the architecture by stepping in instead of letting it hold.

You can give someone perfect four-layer ownership – personal, professional, organisational, cultural – and still undermine it by being the one who answers their questions, makes their decisions, or catches their drift.

The frameworks work. But only if you let them. The Drift Map shows you where you're not letting them.

After all, the architecture can't hold what your identity won't release. And that's the hardest part of this entire journey.

But it's also where freedom begins.

Where to Go Deeper

The Drift Map is a diagnostic tool, not an implementation guide.

It shows you where the architecture is weak and where you're compensating with personal involvement. But building the architecture to fill those gaps requires the frameworks we've covered in Part II.

If the Drift Map reveals gaps, here's where to look for the missing architecture:

Clarity drift → Revisit Role Agreements (Chapter 6)

Alignment drift → Strengthen Oversight Loop rhythms (Chapter 7)

Accountability drift → Build systematic visibility and loops (Chapter 7)

Renewal drift → Protect structural renewal rhythms (Chapter 7)

THE LEADER'S SHIFT

Identity, Pride, Power, and the Architecture of Letting Go

You now have the frameworks: The Architecture Triangle. External Calibration. The Pact. The Oversight Loop. The Drift Map.

These are the structures that make Oversight possible.

Here's what I learned the hard way at Icon: frameworks alone won't set you free. Because every number in your business, every metric you track, every pattern in your data, tells two stories. The first is about what needs to change. The second is about why you haven't changed it yet.

Part III is about that second story.

CHAPTER 9

When the Numbers Talk Back: Reading the Human Story Behind Your Business Data

I want to tell you about a moment that changed how I work with founders.

I was sitting across from two business partners, husband and wife, who ran a creative agency. Good business. Growing. Revenue up almost fifty percent year on year. By most measures, they were winning.

I'd spent two weeks analysing their numbers. Revenue per team member. Staff cost ratios. Operating margins. Recurring versus project revenue. Monthly cash flow patterns. The full picture.

The data was clear. Unambiguous. I could see exactly what was broken and exactly what needed to change.

So I laid it out.

I showed them that despite nearly a million dollars in revenue, their real operating profit was under fifty thousand. I showed them their revenue swung from one hundred and twenty-eight thousand in a good month to forty-three thousand in a bad one. I showed them they were paying themselves thirty thousand dollars below market rate each. I showed them they were spending almost nothing on their own marketing, despite selling marketing for a living.

The numbers were right there. On the screen. In black and white.

They nodded. They understood every data point. They agreed with every conclusion.

And nothing changed.

Not that week. Not the next. Not for months. That's when I realised something I'd missed for twenty years.

Every Number Tells Two Stories

The first story is numerical. Revenue per team member is below benchmark. The operating margin is thin. The revenue mix is too heavily weighted toward project work. The founders are working fifty-five hours a week.

That story is important. It's the diagnostic. It shows you what needs to change.

But there's a second story underneath every number. A human story. And if you don't read that story, the first one doesn't matter. Because the founder who needs to raise their prices but hasn't resolved the impostor syndrome behind their pricing will find twelve reasons not to.

The founder who needs to delegate but whose sense of purpose is built around being indispensable will take back every decision within a month.

The founder who needs to invest in marketing but can't see past the next cash flow crisis will keep telling themselves "next quarter."

The data tells you what is wrong. The emotional pattern tells you why it stays wrong.

And that gap, the space between knowing what to change and being able to change it, is where most business improvement efforts go to die.

The Gap Nobody Talks About

You've probably experienced this yourself. You read something, hear something from an advisor, or see something in your own data, and you think: yes, that's right. That needs to change.

You understand the problem. You can see the solution. You might even know the first three steps.

And you still don't do it.

Not because you're lazy. Not because you lack discipline. Not because your team isn't capable. Because there's an emotional pattern running underneath the operational problem, and until that pattern is addressed, the operational fix won't stick.

I know this because I lived it.

At Icon, I understood the concept of delegation. I'd advised clients on it for years. I could explain the difference between handing over tasks and transferring ownership. I could map accountability frameworks on a whiteboard with my eyes closed.

And I still couldn't let go.

Every time I delegated a client relationship, I'd find myself checking in. Just a quick call. Just to make sure. Every time I handed over a decision, I'd review it afterwards. Not because I didn't trust the person. Because something deeper in me didn't trust that the architecture could hold without my hand on it.

The frameworks I'd built were sound. The problem was me.

And the problem with me wasn't willpower or discipline or knowledge. It was that my sense of purpose had become inseparable from being the person who held everything together.

The numbers would have shown it. Revenue growing, margin flat. Team capable, decisions still flowing through me. Systems in place, founder hours unchanged.

If I'd known how to read the second story, the human story behind those numbers, I would have seen what was really happening years earlier.

The Patterns That Keep Founders Stuck

After working with dozens of founder-led businesses and living through my own version of this, I've come to see that the emotional patterns behind the numbers cluster into recognisable shapes.

In Part II, we explored drift and how to track it. But what I didn't talk about explicitly was the five elements of drift: The Fog, The Shift, The Gap, The Drain, and The Weight. Each represents a structural weakness in the business architecture. But underneath each structural weakness lies an emotional pattern that created it, and that emotional pattern will recreate each weakness again if left unaddressed.

Two of these – The Gap and The Shift – we've already explored. The Gap appeared in Chapter 1: the space between what you think is happening and what's actually happening, where founders unconsciously become the glue. The Shift came in Chapter 2: the move from working IN your business to working ON it.

Here in Part III, we go deeper into the three drifts that show up most visibly in your numbers and in your body: The Fog, The Drain, and The Weight. These are the patterns that data reveals but founders often can't see – because they're too close, too invested, and too exhausted to notice.

Three emotional patterns show up most clearly in the numbers. You'll rarely find just one. Most founders at this stage are running all three at once, and they reinforce each other, which is what makes them so bloody hard to break.

The Undervaluation Pattern

This is the founder who charges too little, pays themselves too little, and invests too little in the future of the business.

In the numbers, it looks like this: revenue per team member sits well below industry benchmarks. Founder salaries are significantly under market rate. Spending on the business's own marketing, training, and development is near zero.

Three separate data points. Same root cause.

The founder doesn't believe the work is worth what the market says it is.

I've seen this pattern in agencies, consulting firms, trade businesses and technology companies. The industry doesn't matter. The pattern is the same.

The founder prices based on what they'd personally be comfortable paying, not what the work delivers. They pay everyone else first and treat their own salary as the variable when cash gets tight. They tell themselves "the business can't afford it" when the truth is "the model hasn't been designed to support it."

And here's what makes this pattern so stubborn: it's masked as market awareness. The founder genuinely believes they're being realistic about pricing. They genuinely believe the business can't afford to pay them more. They genuinely believe that investing in marketing or training is a luxury for businesses bigger than theirs.

They're not lying. They're looking at the data through an emotional lens that distorts everything.

At Icon, I saw a version of this in myself. Not in pricing, our rates were competitive, but in how I thought about investment. Every dollar I considered spending on something that didn't immediately generate revenue felt irresponsible. Training for the team? We'll do it when things settle down. Upgrading our systems? Next quarter. Hiring ahead of demand? Too risky.

I was running a successful agency with a scarcity mindset built in the first year of business, when scarcity was real. The business had grown. The mindset hadn't.

The numbers would have shown it. If I'd looked at what we were spending on our own development as a percentage of revenue and compared it to what we were recommending our clients spend, the gap would have been embarrassing.

But I wasn't reading the second story. I was reading the first story, the numbers, and telling myself they made sense.

This pattern feeds The Fog. When you don't value your own contribution, you struggle to articulate it clearly to others. Role clarity suffers because your sense of what the role is worth remains murky, even to you.

The Volatility Pattern

This is the founder living in survival mode.

In the numbers, it shows up as wild monthly revenue swings, too little recurring income, and operating expenses that consume almost everything the business earns. Multiple loss months in a year despite strong overall revenue. No financial buffer.

The emotional pattern underneath: the founder is operating in permanent threat mode.

When your revenue swings three to one between your best month and your worst, when a forty-six thousand dollar profit in June becomes a nineteen thousand dollar loss in July, your body registers that the same way it registers danger. The amygdala doesn't distinguish between a cash flow crisis and a physical threat.

When you've experienced loss months, even good months don't feel safe. You're always anticipating the next dip.

So you say yes to every piece of work that comes in, regardless of fit. You avoid turning down projects even at razor-thin margins. You check the bank balance every morning. You can't plan beyond thirty days because planning feels pointless when you're one bad month from trouble.

And here's the trap: the reactive behaviour the volatility creates actually perpetuates the volatility.

Saying yes to everything means you never build the recurring revenue base that smooths the cycle. Never investing in marketing means you're always dependent on whatever walks through the door. Never building a cash buffer means every dip triggers crisis mode, which triggers more reactive decisions.

The founder who lives in this pattern knows, intellectually, that they need more recurring revenue. They know they need to be more selective about the work they take on. They know they need a buffer.

But they can't act on what they know. Because acting on it means saying no to revenue that's right in front of them in favour of a structural change that might take six months to materialise.

And when you're in survival mode, six months might as well be six years.

This is The Drain at its most vicious. Your body stays flooded with cortisol. Your decisions stay reactive. Your renewal score stays at two out of ten. And the architecture you're trying to build never gets the breathing room it needs to take hold.

The Founder Overload Pattern

This is the most dangerous pattern because it's the one founders wear as a badge of honour.

In the numbers: the founder works fifty-plus hours a week, every decision flows through them, team accountability scores are low, and if there are co-founders, there's a significant gap in how each one experiences the business.

The emotional pattern underneath: the founder's sense of purpose is built around being the one who holds it all together.

When a founder tells me their team can't make decisions without them, the data usually confirms it. Low accountability scores. High founder hours. Decisions concentrated at the top.

What the data also shows, if you know how to read it, is why.

The team hasn't been given the architecture to make decisions. What's more, the founder hasn't built that architecture because, at some level they may not even be conscious of, building it would mean they're no longer the person the business turns to first. And that role, the person everyone needs, has become how they understand their own value.

This isn't weakness. It's human. And it's invisible to the person inside it.

You can read every chapter in Part II of this book. You can build the Architecture Triangle. You can write four-layer Role Agreements. You can implement the Oversight Loop and complete the Drift Map every week.

And you can still be the one who answers every question, overrides every decision, and catches every piece of drift before the system has a chance to.

Not because the frameworks aren't working, but because the person operating them hasn't yet separated who they are from what they do.

The numbers will show you this is happening in various ways. Founder hours that don't decrease even as systems improve. Decisions that technically belong to someone else but somehow still end up on your desk. A team that's capable on paper but hesitant in practice.

Those numbers are telling you a story about yourself. And it's a harder story to hear than any revenue report.

This is The Weight. The invisible burden of being the person who holds it all together. And until you face why you need to carry it, no amount of delegation training or accountability frameworks will set you free.

The Moment of Recognition

I said at the start of this chapter that I sat across from two founders who understood every data point and still couldn't change.

What I didn't tell you is what eventually did change.

It wasn't a new framework. It wasn't better data. It wasn't a more compelling business case for change.

It was a question.

I asked the co-founder who was working fifty-five hours a week while scoring her own rest at two out of ten: "What would you need to believe about yourself to let someone else carry this?"

She went quiet for a long time.

Then she said: "I'd need to believe I'm still valuable if I'm not the one fixing everything."

That's the second story. Right there. In one sentence.

And until that story changes, no framework, no system, no architecture will hold. Because the founder will unconsciously pull it apart to maintain the version of themselves that feels safe, even when that version is destroying them.

Lifting the Weight

The Weight is an element of drift that is carried uniquely by you as the founder. It's also the element that, when you let it go, will help you overcome the four other elements of drift.

Make no mistake. Removing The Weight you've been carrying is one of the biggest challenges you'll face. It's not just about The Weight itself. It's about the fear of what happens when you put it down. The question of who you are when the business no longer needs you to be the one holding it together.

But you have to find a way to lighten that Weight. It's the hardest, and most important, part of this entire journey.

CHAPTER 10

The Weight and The Zero: The Burden Only Founders Carry

Every founder begins with energy.

Hunger. Belief. The kind of optimism that makes impossible things feel inevitable.

In those early days, the load feels light because it's powered by pure adrenaline and the thrill of building something from nothing.

I remember that feeling at Icon. The first client. The first hire. The first real revenue. Everything felt possible. The Weight of responsibility felt like rocket fuel.

But somewhere along the way, somewhere between year five and year fifteen, The Weight changes. It stops being fuel. It starts being a burden. And most founders never see it happening until they're crushed underneath it.

The data on this is sobering. Depression rates among founders run at multiples of the general population. A troubling number have experienced suicidal thoughts. The average founder works far beyond sustainable hours, with chronic sleep issues and almost no true time off. The full picture is in the Appendix, and it's confronting.

This isn't a character flaw. It's what happens when human beings carry weight the architecture should be carrying.

The Invisible Accumulation

The Weight doesn't arrive suddenly. It builds slowly, quietly, invisibly.

It accumulates in the decisions no one else sees you make. The hard conversations you avoid because you're too drained to have them. The expectations you internalise from your team, your clients, your family, your own ambition.

At Icon, I absorbed every wobble in the organisation. Client unhappy? My fault. Team member struggling? My responsibility. Revenue dipping? My problem to solve.

I told myself this was leadership. This was what founders do. We carry the load so our teams don't have to.

Slowly, imperceptibly, I began to normalise the pressure.

A team member would make a mistake, and instead of letting them own the cleanup, I'd step in to fix it. A client relationship would get tense, and instead of trusting my account director to manage it, I'd take over the conversation. A decision would stall, and instead of pushing ownership back to the person responsible, I'd make the call myself.

I was absorbing the drift of the organisation instead of designing a system to catch it. And I told myself it was for this season. Until we stabilised. Just until the team matured. Or until the market settled.

But the season never ended.

Because when you become the solution to every problem, the problems never stop needing you.

Pause for a moment. When did The Weight stop being temporary for you? Can you name the season that never ended?

When Weight Becomes Identity

The most dangerous part of this journey is when The Weight stops being something you carry and starts being who you are.

I can pinpoint when this happened for me.

It was 2018, maybe early 2019. Icon was at its peak. We were doing huge projects, working with major developers, home builders, and national brands. Revenue was up. The team was strong. On paper, everything looked good.

Yet, I woke up one morning and realised: I couldn't remember the last time I'd felt joy about the business.

I wasn't leading Icon anymore. I was holding Icon.

And then COVID hit. And all the plans I'd been making, the strategies to step back, the succession thinking, the systems I was going to build... All of it went out the window.

Because when crisis hits, founders don't architect. We grip tighter.

My identity had fused with the organisation. When the business was up, I was up. When it wobbled, my sense of self-worth wobbled with it. When a client was unhappy, I didn't just feel responsible, I felt like a failure as a human being.

I wasn't running a company. I was carrying the entire existence of it in my nervous system.

This is what happens when The Weight becomes identity: you stop being a person who leads a business and become a person who IS the business.

Every falter is a threat to your existence.

Every problem is evidence of your inadequacy.

Every request for help feels like proof you're not enough.

And you can't let go. Because if the business doesn't need you to hold it together, who are you?

The Weight No One Else Carries

What makes this weight so isolating is that no one else in your organisation carries it the same way you do.

Every level feels some form of pressure, but not all pressure is created equal. Employees feel the pressure of tasks and deadlines. If they fail, they might lose a job; painful, but recoverable. Managers feel the weight of responsibility for their teams. If they fail, they might damage their reputation; difficult, but repairable. Executives feel the burden of accountability for divisional results. If they fail, they might lose their position; serious, but survivable.

But there is a specific, jagged edge of fear that is reserved solely for the person at the top.

This is what I call The Zero Principle.

The Zero Principle

The Zero is the realisation that sits at the very base of a founder's mind, usually unspoken, often unacknowledged: *If this business fails, it goes to zero. And that zero belongs entirely to me.*

It's not a logical business metric. It's emotional. Visceral. Existential.

While others might lose a job, the founder faces the loss of their identity, their legacy, their financial security, their self-worth, all at once.

The Zero doesn't live in a spreadsheet.

It sits in your chest when you wake up at 3AM.

It sits in your stomach during board meetings.

It shapes your nervous system and influences every decision you make, often without you even realising it.

The Zero is the silent passenger in every strategic conversation, every hiring decision, every client negotiation, every financial choice.

For me, the Zero felt like this: a constant low-grade anxiety that never fully went away, even on good days. A tightness in my chest when I looked at the cash flow projection. A spike of panic when a key employee mentioned wanting to talk. A sinking feeling when I saw a client email come in after hours.

Not because anything was actually wrong. But because everything could go wrong. And if it did, the Zero was waiting.

Sit with this. Where do you feel the Zero in your body right now? The tightness, the vigilance, the thing that never quite goes away?

The Anchor of the Glue

This is what anchors you to The Weight. This is why you can't let go.

Pride whispers a dangerous lie: "No one else can be trusted with the Zero."

When you carry the Zero, you stay "the glue" because you believe, consciously or unconsciously, that if your hands aren't on everything, the risk of hitting Zero increases.

You can't delegate the Zero. You can't outsource the Zero. You can't share the Zero.

So you stay in the middle of everything, convinced that your constant involvement is the only thing preventing collapse.

I remember a conversation with my wife in late 2020, deep into COVID lockdowns. She asked me why I couldn't take a real break, not a working-from-home break, but actual time off.

I said: "If I'm not holding this together right now, it could all fall apart. We could lose everything."

She looked at me and said: "You believe that, don't you? That the entire business will collapse if you stop for even a few days."

And I realised: Yes. I did believe that.

Because COVID had proven what I'd always feared: that when crisis hits, I have to be the one holding everything together. Because I was carrying the Zero alone. And I couldn't imagine the architecture holding it without me.

This fear keeps founders trapped in the "Hero" role. Sacrificing health. Sacrificing relationships. Sacrificing presence with their own lives. Because they feel like they're the only one standing between the business and its end.

The Leaders in Their Cars

I've worked with dozens of founders since selling Icon. And I've heard the same story, told in different ways, again and again.

The leader sitting in their car in the parking lot of their own office, hands gripping the steering wheel, unable to walk inside. Not because they don't care. But because the pressure of the Zero has become too heavy to carry for one more day.

They're exhausted in a way sleep cannot fix.

They're the "database" everyone queries.

They're the "firefighter" who handles every emergency.

They're the "emotional shock absorber" for fifty, eighty, a hundred people.

And they have no one to absorb The Weight for them.

I've been that person in the car. Multiple times. Most memorably in early 2023, about eighteen months after the worst of COVID.

We'd made it through. Revenue was recovering. The team had stabilised. By all external measures, we were on the other side. But I sat there in the parking lot for twenty minutes, staring at the building I'd built, unable to move.

Not because I didn't know what to do. But because I knew that walking through that door meant carrying the Zero for another day. And after three years of crisis management, three years of being the only thing standing between the business and collapse, I didn't know if I had it in me anymore.

That's when I knew something fundamental had to change.

Not the business model. Not the team. Not the market strategy.

Me.

The way I was leading. The way I was carrying. The way I'd built my identity around being Atlas.

This is the question: What would have to change in you – not your business, not your team – for the load to finally lift?

What Oversight Does with the Zero

Here's the truth most business books won't tell you: Oversight doesn't remove the Zero. Nothing can.

As long as you're the founder, that ultimate existential risk remains yours. The business is your responsibility. The outcome is your outcome.

But Oversight does something different: it builds the architecture around the Zero so that you're not crushed by it.

Instead of you being the only person holding back the tide with your bare hands, it becomes the levee. You're still the owner of the outcome. But the system provides the predictability, clarity, and distributed ownership that allow your nervous system to finally stop reacting as if every day is a fight for survival.

Let me be specific about what this means...

Without Oversight:

The Zero sits in your chest every waking moment.

Every decision feels existential.

You can't step away without anxiety spiking.

The business wobbles when you're not in the middle.

Your nervous system stays in permanent fight-or-flight.

With Oversight:

The Zero still exists, but the architecture holds most of the weight.

Most decisions are distributed to clear owners.

You can step away and the system stays aligned.

The business holds its shape because the architecture holds it.

Your nervous system can down-regulate.

This is the shift that changes everything.

When Revenue Becomes Your Worth

For many founders, the Zero isn't about business survival. It's tangled with something deeper: what I call the Money Mirror.

The Money Mirror is the unconscious belief that the numbers on your P&L reflect your value as a human being. Revenue becomes proof that you're enough. Cash flow becomes the measure of your safety. Growth proves you're valuable.

When the business is up, you're up. When revenue dips, your sense of self-worth dips with it. When a deal falls through, it's not a business loss, it feels like evidence of personal inadequacy.

The Zero sits in your chest partly because you've tied your identity to the bank account.

And here's the trap: more money never fixes the mirror.

I discovered this in 2019. Icon was at its financial peak, multiple seven figures in revenue, major clients, strong growth. By every external measure, I should have felt successful.

But I didn't. Because no amount of revenue could fill the hole left by believing that my worth was measured by the numbers.

A good month felt like a temporary reprieve. A slow month felt like an existential threat. Every financial decision became a referendum on my value. And the exhaustion wasn't from running the business. It was from using money as a mirror to prove I was enough, and never quite believing the reflection.

The Architecture of Enough

What Oversight reveals to you is that your worth isn't in the revenue. The architecture holds your value, not the bank account.

Once you separate your identity from the financial outcomes, something profound shifts: you make decisions from wisdom instead of fear. You build from abundance instead of scarcity. You define what "enough" means instead of chasing an ever-moving target.

The architecture doesn't only hold the business weight. It holds the psychological weight of believing money determines your worth.

And when you're no longer using revenue as a mirror, you can finally lead from clarity instead of from the desperate need to prove yourself valuable.

The Zero still exists. But it's no longer measuring your worth as a human being. It's a business reality that the architecture helps you manage.

This separation, between who you are and what the business earns, is one of the deepest shifts Oversight creates.

And it's one of the most liberating.

The Recognition That Changes Everything

Oversight begins with a single, painful recognition:

This weight was never meant to be carried alone.

Not because you're weak. Not because you failed. But because the architecture of "Hero Leadership" is fundamentally unsustainable.

You cannot become the Architect until you stop trying to be Atlas.

The Weight doesn't go away. The Zero doesn't disappear. But when you build the architecture, when you distribute ownership, when you create visibility systems, when you establish accountability loops, when you protect renewal rhythms, the pressure moves from your shoulders to the structure.

And for the first time since you started this journey, you can breathe. This is what Part III is about: the psychological shift required to stop being the glue.

Because the frameworks in Part II only work if you're willing to do the identity work in Part III.

The architecture can't hold what your identity isn't willing to release. This is the biggest challenge on the road to implementing Oversight.

But it's also where you find freedom.

CHAPTER 11

The Inner Shift: Fear, Grief, and Becoming the Architect

There's a moment in every founder's journey when the architecture is built, the team is capable, and the systems are holding, yet you can't let go.

I remember mine.

It was a Tuesday afternoon, three months before I sold Icon. The business was running smoothly. Decisions were being made without me. The Oversight Loop was catching drift. By every measure, the architecture was working.

And I was terrified.

Not of failure. Of success.

If the business truly didn't need me anymore, who was I?

The Fear of Empty Space

That question sat in my chest like the Zero itself. For twenty years, my identity had been fused with Icon. I was the founder who made things happen. The one who caught every falling ball. The person everyone turned to when things got hard.

Letting go meant confronting a terrifying possibility: that the space I'd been filling wasn't essential. That the business could breathe without my constant presence. That my worth wasn't measured by how much I carried.

The fear whispered constantly. What if the team falters without you watching? What if quality slips? What if clients notice you're not as involved? What if everything you built unravels the moment you step back?

I know now that this fear is universal. Every founder who builds real architecture faces it. The nervous system, trained on years of adrenaline, rebels against rest. The identity, constructed around being needed, fights against becoming optional.

But I also learned something else: the fear is a doorway, not a wall.

When I finally took a full week offline – no email, no calls, no checking in – the business didn't collapse. It wobbled slightly, then steadied. Problems arose and got solved. Decisions were made. The architecture held.

And I sat with the strangest feeling: relief mixed with grief.

The Grief of the Hero

The relief made sense. The grief surprised me.

I was mourning something I hadn't expected to miss: being indispensable.

For two decades, my worth had been tied to how much the business needed me. Every crisis I solved, every decision I made, every gap I filled: these were proof that I mattered. The exhaustion was brutal, but it was also validating. If I was this tired, I must be really important.

Letting go meant releasing that validation. It meant accepting that my value wasn't in the carrying, but in what I'd built that could carry itself.

This is what I've come to call the Hero's Death: the quiet moment when the founder identity that served you for years finally breaks. Not dramatically. Not catastrophically. But in the pause where you used to intervene but now trust the architecture. In the silence where you used to fill every gap but now let the system breathe.

I grieved the hero I'd been. The one who worked until midnight. The one everyone depended on. The one who secretly loved being the answer to every problem.

That version of me had to die for the Architect to emerge.

The Separation

The deepest work wasn't strategic. It was psychological.

I had to separate my identity from the business.

For years, Icon wasn't just something I'd built: it was who I was. When the business succeeded, I succeeded. When it struggled, I struggled. Every client win felt like personal validation. Every setback felt like personal failure.

This fusion had driven the early growth. My intensity, my standards, my relentless involvement: these had shaped the culture and built the reputation.

But what accelerates growth in the early years becomes a ceiling later. When you and the business are one, the organisation is capped by your personal bandwidth. Your nervous system becomes the company's nervous system. Your limitations become its limitations.

The separation wasn't about caring less. It was about caring differently.

I learned to say: "I built this business, but I am not this business. Its success doesn't prove my worth. Its struggles don't diminish me. I am the Architect, not the architecture."

This sounds simple. It took me months to believe it.

What I Found on the Other Side

The Hero's Death isn't loss. It's liberation.

On the other side, I discovered something unexpected: I was more valuable to Icon as an Architect than I'd ever been as the hero.

As the hero, I was the ceiling. Every decision waited for me. Every problem needed my input. The business could only grow as fast as I could personally manage.

As the Architect, I was the foundation. The systems I'd built could scale without me. The team could grow beyond my bandwidth. The culture could sustain itself when I wasn't in the room.

And I got something back I'd forgotten existed: myself.

Not the exhausted founder running on adrenaline. Not the hero defined by being needed. But the person I'd been before the business consumed everything: curious, creative, present.

I started sleeping through the night. I stopped waking with anxiety. I found myself thinking about possibilities instead of problems. The business hadn't needed me to be the glue for months. And instead of making me irrelevant, it made me human again.

The Quiet Truth

If you're building this architecture, if you're doing the work of Oversight, you'll face this moment too.

The systems will start holding. The team will start owning. And you'll feel the fear rise up: *what if I'm not needed anymore?*

Let me offer what I wish someone had told me:

The fear is real, but it's not prophetic.

The architecture can hold. Trust it enough to test it.

The grief is real, but it's not permanent. You're not losing yourself. You're becoming someone who doesn't need exhaustion to feel valuable.

The separation is real, but it's not cold. You can love what you've built without being consumed by it. You can care deeply and still have boundaries.

And on the other side is something worth the journey: a life that fits, a business that stands, and a version of yourself you might have forgotten existed.

The hero's death is where the Architect is born.

When you're ready, the architecture will be waiting.

CHAPTER 12

The First 90 Days, When Honest Reflection Becomes Architecture

The first 90 days of Oversight are not primarily operational. They're emotional.

More specifically, they're about reflection. Real reflection. The kind that requires you to look honestly at where you are, how you got here, and what you've been carrying that the business should be carrying.

This is harder than it sounds.

Because to understand where clarity is missing, you first have to understand your role in creating the confusion. To see where ownership is blurred, you have to see where you've been the one blurring it. To recognise drift, you have to acknowledge your complicity in allowing it.

The first 90 days require something most founders resist: brutal honesty about yourself.

Not judgement. Not shame. Not beating yourself up for what you've done wrong.

But an honest assessment of where the pain has left scars. What patterns you've built to survive. What weight you're carrying that you never intended to pick up. Where you've become the glue without realising it was happening.

Defensiveness in this phase is fatal.

Every founder has skeletons. Every founder has made mistakes. Every founder has built dependencies they didn't mean to create.

The question isn't whether you've done this. You have. We all have.

The question is: can you see it clearly enough to change it?

You Cannot Do This Alone

In the previous chapter, we explored identity separation, the moment you realise you are not the business, you are the Architect of the business. That realisation changes everything. But it's not the end of the journey. It's the beginning.

Because knowing you need to separate your identity from the business and actually doing the work to separate it are two very different things.

This chapter is about that work. The emotional journey you'll travel as you move from glue to Architect. What it feels like to begin.

The uncomfortable truth, as I've shared already, is you cannot see your own drift while you're inside it.

And you cannot navigate this journey of honest reflection without someone who understands what you're going through. Someone who has been through it themselves. Someone who can hold the mirror steady when you're shaking.

Not a compliance advisor. Not someone who just validates your decisions. But someone who can see what you're protecting and help you examine it without judgement.

Let me be direct about something: our success is always built on the back of our learning moments. And our greatest learning moments are full of pain and scars.

The mistakes you've made. The dependencies you've created. The patterns that nearly broke you. Those aren't things to hide. They're the raw material of wisdom.

But you need someone who can help you look at those scars without shame. Someone who has their own scars and can say: "I see what you're carrying. I've carried it too. Let me share what helped."

This is why External Calibration isn't optional. It's essential. That's why it's the first pillar of Oversight.

In my journey, I needed the consultant to tell me what I couldn't see. I needed someone outside my system who could say: "You've built a business that only works when you're the glue. And that's not sustainable."

For you, it might be a coach. A peer who's been through this. A consultant trained in Oversight. Someone from Two Icons who can guide you through this architecture.

But whoever it is, they need to have walked this road. Because the first 90 days aren't a checklist. They're an emotional journey. And you need someone who knows the terrain.

A Note on Timing: Don't Rush This

Before we go further, I need to say something crucial: the "90 days" isn't a deadline. It's a framework for understanding the emotional phases you'll move through.

Some founders need 60 days. Some need 120. Some need longer.

The timeline doesn't matter. What matters is that you don't rush the reflection.

This is the most crucial phase of the entire Oversight journey. If you skip the honest assessment in Phase 1 because you're impatient to "implement solutions," you'll build architecture on a foundation of denial. And it won't hold.

Take the time you need. Sit with the discomfort. Look at the patterns. Examine the scars.

The rest of Oversight depends on this foundation.

So don't measure success by how quickly you move through these phases. Measure it by how honestly you navigate them.

Because honest reflection; a real, vulnerable, unflinching examination of where you are and how you got here; is where transformation actually begins.

Not in the frameworks. Not in the Role Agreements. Not in the Oversight Loop.

In the moment you finally see yourself clearly and decide to change.

What to Expect Emotionally

Rather than give you a prescriptive timeline, let me show you what these phases feel like. What emotions to expect. How to know you're moving through them authentically. Because the timeline matters less than the emotional honesty of the journey.

The transition unfolds in three distinct emotional phases. And each one requires something different from you.

Phase One: Exposure

The Emotion: "I didn't realise how much I was carrying"

This phase is about visibility. But more than that, it's about honesty.

As you begin to map the architecture, document Role Agreements, run the Drift Map, and establish the Oversight Loop, you're not creating frameworks. You're being forced to see what you've been avoiding.

The drift you've normalised. The dependency you've created. The pressure you've been carrying alone. The decisions you make that no one else is allowed to make. The conversations you avoid because you're too tired to have them.

This phase feels raw because you're not fixing anything yet. You're just seeing it clearly. All of it. Without the stories you tell yourself about why it has to be this way.

Take the time you need here. This isn't a race. Some founders spend weeks in this phase. Some spend months. The timeline doesn't matter. What matters is that you see it honestly.

A note for the exhausted: If you're reading this and thinking "I'm too tired to even begin this work", that's exactly where Oversight starts. In the empty. When you're post-collapse and energy is gone.

The Weight's final trick is convincing you that change is impossible when you're at your lowest. But the truth is: the architecture holds even when you can't. It's designed for the exhausted founder.

You don't need energy to begin. You need to name one thing. One glue moment you're tired of being. One question from the Drift Map. One Sacred Pause of ten minutes to breathe.

Start there. The architecture will hold you first, before you hold anything else.

You are not too far gone. Begin here.

What's crucial to know: defensiveness will kill this phase before it begins.

When you see that your team doesn't own outcomes, the instinct is to blame them: "They don't step up. They wait for me to decide everything."

But honest reflection asks: Why do they wait? What have I done to teach them that waiting is safer than deciding?

When you see that communication is unclear, the instinct is to think: "They should know this by now."

But honest reflection asks: Have I actually made it clear? Or have I kept it in my head and expected them to read my mind?

As you see drift everywhere, the instinct is panic: "This is worse than I thought. I need to fix all of this immediately."

But honest reflection says: This didn't happen overnight. It happened slowly, over years. I can't fix it overnight either. First, I need to see it clearly.

Defensiveness looks for someone to blame. Honest reflection looks for patterns to understand.

And the first 90 days only work if you choose reflection over defence.

My first 30 days:

I started by running the Drift Map on myself. Four questions, brutal honesty.

Where is communication becoming unclear? Everywhere. My team was asking me to clarify decisions that should have been obvious from their roles.

I had to admit: I'd never actually made those roles clear. I'd kept strategy in my head, assuming they'd figure it out. Then I'd get frustrated when they asked for clarity I'd never provided.

Where is culture wobbling? Any time I wasn't in the room. The values held when I modelled them, wavered when I didn't.

I had to admit: I'd built a culture that depended on my personal presence instead of systematic rituals. I was the culture. And that was my choice, my pattern, my failure to build structure.

Where is accountability blurring? I was the only one following up on commitments. The team waited for me to catch what slipped.

I had to admit: I'd trained them to wait. Every time something slipped and I caught it, I reinforced the pattern that I was the safety net. They didn't own accountability because I'd never let them experience the consequences of not owning it.

Where is my capacity depleting? I was working sixty-hour weeks and hadn't taken a real day off in eighteen months.

I had to admit: I chose this. I wore exhaustion as proof of dedication. I filled every gap because being needed felt like being valuable. My burnout wasn't something that happened to me, it was something I created by refusing to let go.

Writing this down, seeing it on paper without the defensive stories, felt like being punched in the chest.

Not because my team had failed. But because I'd built a system that required me to be the glue, then resented being trapped by what I'd built.

The consultant had been right: none of my people owned anything.

I was the one who'd made it that way.

What to do in Phase 1:

• Run the Drift Map weekly. Don't fix anything yet, just observe where

you're the glue.

• Document what's really happening vs. what you thought was happening

(the Oversight Gap).

• Start drafting Role Agreements, but don't implement them yet. Map

who should own what.

• Tell your team what you're doing: "I'm building architecture so this

business can grow without me being in everything."

What to expect:

Overwhelm. You'll see gaps everywhere. Resist the urge to fix them all immediately.

Guilt. You'll realise how much dependency you've created. That's okay. You didn't know.

Resistance. Your nervous system will scream that seeing problems without fixing them is dangerous. Ignore it.

What's hard:

Not stepping in. When you see drift, every instinct says, "fix it now." But in Phase 1, your job is to observe, not rescue.

Looking at your skeletons. Every founder has mistakes they'd rather not examine. Decisions that created dependency. Patterns that enabled dysfunction. Pain that left scars you've been protecting. Phase 1 asks you to look at all of it without judgement. Make an honest assessment.

Admitting you're the problem. Not the market. Not the team. Not bad luck. You. The way you've led. The dependencies you've created. The architecture you've failed to build. This is the hardest admission most founders will ever make.

What matters:

Clarity before action. You can't build architecture until you see what's missing. Phase 1 is about seeing it clearly.

Phase Two: Redistribution

The Emotion: "I don't have to carry this alone"

In this phase, the architecture begins to take the strain.

This is when you implement Role Agreements and build the Human Architecture. When you start the Oversight Loop rhythms. When ownership shifts from you to the people who should be holding it.

And this is when the withdrawal wobble happens.

My experience in this phase:

I sat down with my Head of Client Services and showed her the Role Agreement I'd drafted.

"You own client retention and satisfaction," I said. "Success is measured by ninety-five percent retention and NPS above fifty. You have full authority over client communication, service delivery, and resource allocation."

She stared at it for a long moment. Then said: "What if I screw it up?"

"Then we'll see it in the metrics and adjust," I told her. "But you've been doing this work for eight years. You just haven't had permission to own it."

Two weeks later, a major client sent an angry email about a delayed deliverable. My immediate instinct was to take over the relationship, fix it myself, make sure it didn't escalate.

Instead, I forwarded it to her with one line: "You own this. Let me know how you handle it."

I spent the next three hours in low-grade panic, checking my email every ten minutes, fighting the urge to step in.

She handled it. Called the client. Acknowledged the delay. Offered a solution. Followed up personally. The client stayed. The relationship got stronger, not weaker.

The wobble I was feeling wasn't the business failing. It was my nervous system adjusting to not being needed.

What to do in Phase 2:

Implement Role Agreements one at a time. Don't try to redistribute everything at once.

Start weekly Oversight Loop meetings (30 minutes, three questions: What do you own this week? Where are you stuck? What decisions need clarity?).

When drift surfaces, coach the owner through solving it instead of solving it yourself.

Protect one Sacred Pause per week (three hours of thinking time, no meetings, no email).

What to expect:

Team uncertainty. They've learned to wait for you. When you push ownership back, they'll be confused at first.

Withdrawal makes the business become unstable. Things will feel shakier, not stabler. That's normal. The system is learning to stand.

Your panic. Every wobble will trigger your fight-or-flight. You'll want to step back in. Don't.

What's hard:

Not rescuing. When your team hesitates or makes a mistake, every instinct says, "I should do it myself." That's the pattern you're breaking.

Tolerating imperfection. They won't do it exactly how you would. That's okay. Outcome ownership means they get to solve it their way.

Coaching instead of doing. It's slower. It feels riskier. But it's the only way the architecture learns to hold.

What matters:

The wobble isn't failure. It's the system learning to stand without you holding it. Don't step back in. Coach through it.

Phase Three: Renewal

The Emotion: "I can breathe again"

In this phase, the shift becomes existential.

The architecture starts to hold its own weight. The team starts to make decisions you used to make. The business begins to function without your constant intervention.

And you, for the first time in years, start to feel space.

My experience in this phase:

In February 2023, after moving through Exposure and Redistribution, two things happened within 48 hours that showed me the architecture was starting to hold.

First, my Head of Client Services saved a major client account, a six-figure relationship that was threatening to leave. It was a critical situation. She renegotiated terms. Strengthened the relationship. Did it all without me.

When she told me afterward, I asked: "Why didn't you escalate this to me?"

She said: "Because I own retention. This was mine to solve."

She talked me through what she'd done. It was better than how I would have handled it because she knew the relationship so deeply. That's when I knew the architecture was starting to hold.

The second thing that happened was I took my first full day off in three years. I told the team I was completely unreachable for 24 hours.

I spent the whole day waiting for the panic to hit. Waiting for the business to need me. Waiting for proof that I couldn't step away.

It never came.

The business operated. Decisions got made. Problems got solved. The world didn't end.

And I sat in my backyard for the first time in years, not thinking about Icon. Just\... breathing.

That's when I knew something fundamental had shifted.

Not that the business was perfect. Not that every role was fully owned. Not that drift had disappeared. But that the architecture was holding enough of The Weight that I wasn't carrying all of it anymore.

What to do in Phase 3:

Expand Sacred Pauses to weekly (half-day) and monthly (full day).

Review Drift Map monthly instead of weekly. The architecture should be catching most drift now.

Celebrate wins with the team: "You owned this outcome and delivered it without me. That's exactly what we're building."

Start thinking strategically again (you'll have capacity for it now).

What to expect:

Moments of space. You'll have your first experience in years of not being needed constantly. It will feel strange, possibly uncomfortable.

Energy returning. You'll sleep better. Think clearer. Feel lighter.

Team confidence rising. They'll start making decisions faster, asking you less, owning outcomes more visibly.

What's hard:

Trusting it's real. The first moments of space will feel fragile. You'll worry it's temporary. It might be at first, but it's also the beginning.

Not filling the space. When you have capacity, the instinct is to fill it with more work. Don't. Use it to think, create, renew.

Letting yourself feel it. After years of exhaustion, space can feel unfamiliar, even wrong. Let yourself adjust.

What matters:

Notice the shift. The business isn't perfect, but it's holding more than it was. You're carrying less than you were. That's progress.

Reinforce the architecture. When something works, name it. When the team owns something well, celebrate it. When you have space, protect it.

What Changes in These Early Phases

By the time I reached the Renewal phase, Icon wasn't magically transformed. But it was fundamentally different.

My team was making most of the decisions I used to make. The reason wasn't that I'd taught them what to decide, but that the architecture made clear what they owned.

Drift was getting caught in weekly loops instead of months later when it became a crisis.

I was working less but achieving more. The architecture was doing work that used to require my personal involvement.

And I could finally see the horizon. Not just the fire in front of me, but the future I was building toward.

The journey took longer than 90 days. It took about five months from first honest reflection to the decision to sell Icon. Not because the business was failing. But because the business was functioning without me, and I could see that clearly because the Oversight architecture gave me the vantage point.

Your timeline will be different. That's okay. What matters is that you don't rush the most crucial phase: honest reflection about where you are and how you got here.

A Founder's Journey Through These Phases

I worked with a founder, let's call him Adam, through these three emotional phases.

Phase 1 – Exposure: He ran the Drift Map and was devastated. "I thought I was building leaders," he told me. "But I'm handing out tasks and calling it delegation."

He spent three weeks sitting with this realisation. Looking at the patterns. Examining where his need for control had created the dependency. No fixing. Just honest assessment.

Phase 2 – Redistribution: He implemented Role Agreements with his leadership team. His CFO pushed back: "If I own cash flow, does that mean I can make decisions about payment terms without asking you?"

Adam's instinct was to say no. Instead, he said: "Yes. Within the boundaries we define together."

A few weeks later, the CFO renegotiated terms with a major supplier, improving cash flow by fifteen percent. Adam never would have thought of that approach.

Phase 3 – Renewal: Adam took his first vacation in four years. Five days offline. When he came back, the business had grown. Two major deals closed. One customer issue resolved. Zero fires.

He told me: "I kept waiting for proof that they needed me. Instead, I got proof that the architecture works."

His journey took about four months from start to finish. Not 90 days. And that's okay. Because six months later, his business grew twenty-two percent while his hours dropped to thirty-five per week. The architecture was holding. And he was finally living.

Common Mistakes in These Early Phases

Mistake 1: Trying to do this alone

You cannot see your own drift from inside it. You need someone who understands this journey, who has their own scars, who can hold the mirror steady. External Calibration isn't optional. It's essential.

Mistake 2: Rushing the reflection phase

This is the most crucial phase of the entire journey. If you skip honest assessment because you're impatient to implement solutions, you'll build on denial. Take the time you need. Weeks or months, whatever it requires.

Mistake 3: Trying to change everything at once

Start with one Role Agreement. One Oversight Loop rhythm. One Sacred Pause per week. Let the architecture build incrementally.

Mistake 4: Stepping back in at the first sign things become unstable

The wobble is the system learning. If you rescue it, you teach dependency. Coach through it instead.

Mistake 5: Not communicating the shift to your team

Tell them what you're building and why. "I'm creating architecture so this business can grow without me being the bottleneck. That means you'll own more, and I'll coach more."

Mistake 6: Measuring success by timeline instead of honesty

The question isn't "Am I on day 47?" The question is "Am I being honest about what I'm seeing?" Emotional honesty matters more than calendar days.

What's Possible When You Navigate This Honestly

These early phases don't fix everything. But they prove something crucial: the architecture can hold. Not perfectly. Not completely. But enough that you're no longer the only thing preventing collapse.

As you move through these phases with honest reflection, when you take the time you need, when you have the external guidance you need, when you're willing to look at your scars without defensiveness, you'll reach a point where:

• The Pact integrates ownership with who people actually are as
individuals.

• Oversight Loop rhythms catch drift weekly.

• Your team makes decisions you used to make.

• You have capacity for strategic thinking you haven't had in years.

• You have proof that stepping back doesn't mean falling apart.
And you'll have crossed the threshold from firefighting to architecting.

From being the glue to building the system.

From carrying everything to trusting the hold.

The Moment You Become the Architect

There is a moment, quiet, subtle, almost sacred, when you finally realise the shift has happened.

It isn't marked by a grand announcement or a financial milestone. Instead, it's found in the stillness of a Monday morning where the phone doesn't ring with a crisis. Or in a boardroom meeting where decisions are made with clarity and confidence without you having to speak a word.

The Death of the Martyr

In this moment, the old versions of your leadership identity begin to fall away.

You realise with profound relief that you are no longer the glue. No longer the bottleneck that every decision must pass through. No longer the firefighter, exhausted from chasing the same flames day after day.

Most importantly, you are no longer the martyr.

The Birth of the Architect

You have become the Architect.

Where there was once adrenaline, there is now architecture. Where there was once chaos, there is now design.

When the architecture holds:

• The culture breathes. It is no longer a fragile "vibe" you have to

manufacture through your personal presence. It is a self-sustaining

system, reinforced by rituals and protected by clarity.

• The team leads. People step into the outcomes they own. They make decisions. They solve problems. They build the business with you,

not for you.

• The business stands. The organisation becomes resilient. Not dependent on your proximity but strengthened by the architecture

you've built.

The journey doesn't end here. But it begins with honest reflection.

With the courage to look at where the pain left scars.

With the humility to admit you can't do this alone.

With the patience to take the time this crucial phase requires.

With space you didn't think you'd ever feel again.

With the first breath of freedom after years of holding your breath.

The architecture is holding.

And so are you.

Just differently than before.

Better than before.

Finally, sustainably, free.

THE NEW WORLD OF LEADERSHIP

Why Oversight Is the Architecture the Future Demands

So far we've covered the personal benefits of Oversight and the work you'll need to do in your own business and your own psyche to lighten The Weight you're carrying. But what about how your business fits into the world as a whole?

You see, Oversight isn't just a framework to help founders share the load and step out of working IN their businesses. It's a framework that builds businesses that can withstand the instability of an uncertain world.

When you become the Architect, you are building to last. Building for the future. Building a business that can not only thrive without you, but navigate change in whatever form it takes.

The chapters in Part IV are about how you can use Oversight to build your legacy on solid foundations.

CHAPTER 13

The Architect: Leadership That Lasts Beyond Disruption

The world has changed. And it will keep changing.

Not just because of the pandemic that forced us to rethink how work happens. Not because of AI that's accelerating what's possible. But because the fundamental contract between leaders and teams has shifted, and it's not shifting back.

Your team no longer accepts leadership by proximity. They expect meaning, not management. They expect clarity, not just presence. They expect systems that protect them, not heroes who rescue them.

Most founders miss this: the shift isn't a threat to your leadership. It's an invitation to claim a role that's more powerful, more sustainable, and more enduring than the one you've been draining yourself to maintain.

The question isn't whether the old way of leading will work. It won't.

The question is: what kind of leader will you become in this new world?

When External Disruption Exposes Internal Fragility

2020 made this clear. COVID didn't create Icon's fragility. It exposed it.

The data confirms this: founder stress levels have risen dramatically since 2019, with hybrid and remote leadership challenges cited as a primary accelerator. Meanwhile, the rapid pace of technological change, AI in particular, has compounded decision fatigue for founders everywhere.

The old playbook isn't failing. It's accelerating the collapse.

For years, our culture had been held together by proximity, the energy of being in the same space, the casual conversations that kept alignment, the osmosis of values through daily interaction.

When proximity disappeared overnight, the architecture underneath was revealed. And there wasn't much there.

Values on a poster. Systems in my head. Decisions waiting for me to make them. Culture dependent on my physical presence to hold its shape.

The business wobbled. Not because the team was incapable. But because I'd built a system that only worked when I was in the middle of it.

This is what external disruption does: it reveals what's holding your business together.

And if the answer is "you," then the disruption doesn't just affect operations. It threatens existence.

The Pattern That Keeps Repeating

Here's what I've observed working with founders since selling Icon...

External disruption – whether it's a pandemic, technological shift, market change, or industry upheaval – doesn't create new problems. It accelerates existing ones.

If your team was already unclear about ownership, hybrid work makes it worse.

If your culture was already fragile, remote interaction makes it falter.

If you were already the bottleneck, distributed teams make you even more essential, and more worn down.

The founders who survive disruption aren't the ones who had perfect systems before the change hit. They're the ones who built architecture that could flex with change instead of depending on stability.

They weren't held together by proximity. They were held together by clarity.

They weren't sustained by the founder's presence. They were sustained by structural design.

And when the world shifted, their businesses adapted, because the architecture could hold new shapes without the founder having to rebuild everything personally.

What AI Actually Changes (And What It Doesn't)

Let me be direct about AI, because I see founders making the same mistake with it that they make with every technological shift: they think it's about the technology.

It's not. It's about what the technology reveals.

AI is exceptional at optimising workflows, analysing data, automating repetitive tasks; all the things that used to consume founder bandwidth. And that's valuable.

But here's what AI cannot do and never will: it cannot sense cultural drift before it becomes an urgent situation. It cannot rebuild trust after a hard season. It cannot inspire a team to protect something greater than themselves.

AI can handle the resource management. But it can't do the cultural stewardship.

And this is the shift that defines the modern Architect: understanding the division between what can be systematised and what must be human.

I watched a founder, we'll call him Mark, spend six months building AI tools to "solve" his operational challenges. Revenue tracking automated. Client communication templated. Workflow optimisation maximised.

And his team became more disengaged than ever.

Why? Because he'd optimised the mechanical without addressing the human. He'd automated tasks without clarifying ownership. He'd systematised activity without building meaning.

AI didn't solve his leadership problem. It made the absence of leadership architecture more obvious.

The Architect understands: technology handles the repeatable. Leadership handles the irreplaceable. Your role isn't to compete with AI at optimisation. Your role is to design the human architecture that AI can serve but never replace.

The End of Leadership by Proximity

For decades, founder-centric leadership worked through physical presence. You could walk the floor and sense the energy. You could have hallway conversations that kept alignment. You could model culture through your daily behaviour and trust that osmosis would spread it.

Proximity masked architectural gaps. If something was unclear, people could just ask you. If culture shook, your presence stabilised it. If ownership blurred, you could step in immediately.

But proximity is no longer reliable. And the truth is it never really was, it was just convenient. Now teams are distributed. Work is hybrid. The office is one location among many, not the centre of gravity.

And what this shift reveals is uncomfortable: if your culture only works when everyone's in the same room, you don't have culture. You have your personal charisma extended across physical space.

If your systems only function when you're physically present to clarify, intervene, and decide, you don't have systems. You have you.

The Architect doesn't mourn the loss of proximity. The Architect builds clarity that travels.

The Rise of Structural Intentionality

The leaders who thrive in this environment, and in whatever disruption comes next, are the ones who shift from proximity-based leadership to architecture-based leadership.

This is what I call Structural Intentionality: designing clarity into the system instead of relying on your presence to create it.

It means:

• Culture becomes designed, not osmotic. Values aren't absorbed

through proximity. They're built into rituals, reinforced through

accountability loops, protected by systematic visibility.

• Ownership becomes distributed, not centralised. Authority flows to

those who own outcomes, regardless of where they sit. The Pact makes

clear what each person owns, how success is measured, what decisions

they can make, and why the work matters to them.

• Accountability becomes systematic, not personal. The Oversight Loop

surfaces drift early through structured rhythms, weekly alignment,

monthly review, quarterly recalibration. You're not chasing

problems. The architecture catches them.

At Icon, I learned this transition the hard way. I went from walking around the office and "feeling" the culture to building rituals that protected culture whether I was in the room or not. From having my team ask me questions in person to documenting Role Agreements that answered those questions systematically. From catching drift through proximity to building the Drift Map that surfaced it through structured reflection.

The architecture didn't replace my leadership. It amplified it beyond my physical presence.

What Changes (And What Doesn't)

Here's what's changing and what will keep changing:

• The tools we use. Technology accelerates. AI capabilities expand.

Communication platforms evolve. The specific tools will keep

shifting.

• The way we work. Hybrid, remote, distributed, the physical

configuration of work will continue to flex with cultural

expectations and technological capability.

• The speed of change. Markets move faster. Industries disrupt

quicker. What worked last year might not work next year.

Here's what doesn't change:

• People need clarity. They need to know what they own, how success is

measured, what authority they have. This doesn't change with

technology or location.

• Culture needs architecture. Values without systematic reinforcement

are just aspirations. Rituals protect meaning regardless of where

people work.

• Drift is constant. The pull back toward the founder as the centre of

gravity never stops. Only architecture resists it.

• Founders need space. You can't lead strategically when you're

drowning operationally. This is true whether you're in an office or working remotely, whether AI exists or not.

The Architect builds on what's timeless, not what's trending.

From Exhausted Centre to Enduring Design

The shift from hero to Architect isn't about working less. It's about building differently.

The hero leads through personal intervention. The Architect leads through systematic design.

The hero's value is in being needed. The Architect's value is in building what lasts beyond being needed.

The hero measures success by hours worked and fires fought. The Architect measures success by what holds when they step away.

I made this shift at Icon in 2022–2023. And it was terrifying. Because being needed felt like being valuable. And stepping back felt like becoming irrelevant.

The opposite was true.

As I was the hero, my value was capped by my personal bandwidth. The business could only grow as much as I could personally carry.

When I became the Architect, my value multiplied through the systems I built. The business could grow beyond my capacity because the architecture held more than I ever could alone.

The hero creates dependency. The Architect creates capability.

The hero builds a job they can never leave. The Architect builds an asset that can stand without them.

This isn't retreat. This is evolution.

The Leader the Future Demands

The world will keep changing. Technology will keep accelerating. Markets will keep disrupting. The founders who survive won't be the ones who work the hardest or react the fastest.

They'll be the ones who build architecture that flexes with change instead of breaking under it. Who design clarity that travels instead of depending on proximity. Who distribute ownership instead of centralising control. Who create systems that catch drift instead of personally chasing every problem.

You don't need to predict the next disruption. You need to build architecture that can handle disruption without requiring you to be the glue holding it together.

That's what the Architect does.

Not because the old way of leading was wrong. But because the world has changed in ways that make the old way unsustainable. And because there's a better way. One that doesn't require your fatigue as the price of success.

The age of the hero is ending. It wasn't that heroes failed. It was that the architecture they neglected to build couldn't scale with the complexity of the modern world.

The age of the Architect has begun.

And it's yours to claim.

Not by working harder. But by building what lasts.

CHAPTER 14

The Leader Who Builds What Lasts

In the final accounting of a career, I've come to believe leadership isn't measured by the intensity of your effort or the hours you spent in the trenches. It's not measured by how much you carried or how many fires you personally extinguished.

It's measured by one thing: what did you build that could stand without you?

The Trap I Almost Fell Into

For years, I believed that being indispensable was the ultimate sign of success. I took pride in the fact that "nothing happens without me." I wore my exhaustion as a badge of dedication. I measured my value by how much the business needed me.

It took me a long time to see what that really meant: I hadn't built an asset. I'd built a high-stakes job I could never leave.

And there's a massive, often invisible, financial cost to this.

The Valuation Gap

In the world of mergers and acquisitions, a business where the founder is the primary hub of all knowledge and decision-making is a high-risk asset.

Because the value walks out the door when you do.

Buyers discount heavily for what's called "key person risk", which is the risk that the business can't function without the founder.

The numbers are stark: founder-dependent businesses sell at significantly lower multiples, a gap that can mean millions of dollars in lost value on mid-market exits. The vast majority of businesses with 10–50 employees aren't considered "exit-ready" without major founder dependency restructuring. And most founders planning an exit worry most about "what happens when I'm not there."

Founder-centric businesses often fetch 2–3x multiples of earnings. The buyer is essentially purchasing a revenue stream that requires them to immediately replace the founder's operational role, which is expensive and risky.

Architecture-centric businesses, those running on Oversight, can command 5–7x multiples or higher. The systems are documented, ownership is distributed, culture is systematic, and the business can transition to new leadership without operational collapse.

The difference between a 3x and a 6x multiple on a \$2M EBITDA business? \$6 million.[5]

That's the cost of being the connective tissue.

The Icon Decision

When I first considered selling Icon, I had a choice.

I could sell it as it had been for most of twenty years: a founder-dependent agency where Joe was the brand, the relationship holder, the primary decision-maker, and the cultural centre.

Or I could sell it as what I'd spent the previous years building: an architecture-centric business where Oversight held the culture, Role Agreements distributed ownership supported by Human Architecture, and the Oversight Loop caught drift systematically.

The first option would have been easier in the short term. But it would have massively discounted the valuation.

The second option required me to do the hardest work of my career: building the architecture that made me unnecessary.

What happened:

The buyer's due diligence didn't just look at our revenue and client retention. They looked at our operational independence from me.

They interviewed the team without me present. They reviewed our Role Agreements. They examined our Oversight Loop

---

5 EBITDA stands for Earnings Before Interest, Taxes, Depreciation, and Amortisation – the standard measure buyers use to value a business. A "3x multiple" means the buyer pays three times your annual EBITDA to acquire the company.

documentation. They tested whether decisions could be made without escalating to the founder.

And they concluded: this business can function without Joe.

That conclusion wasn't a rejection of my value. It was validation that I'd built something more valuable than my personal involvement.

The multiple reflected it.

What I Got Back

What I didn't expect was that the return wasn't just financial.

It was personal.

When you're the glue, your brain is trapped in a constant fight-or-flight response. Every message could be a crisis. Every decision waits for you. Your nervous system never gets to down-regulate.

When the architecture holds, you finally have what I call "strategic bandwidth": the mental capacity to think years ahead instead of hours ahead. To imagine what you could build instead of maintaining what exists.

Nine months after I started building Oversight at Icon, I had my first experience of this in years. I was sitting in a café, not checking email, not putting out fires, just thinking. And I realised: I could see the next three years clearly. Not as a vague hope, but as a designed path.

That's when Two Icons started forming in my mind. Not as a reaction to Icon failing, but as a creation born from having space to think.

The Return of Presence

For years, I was physically present but mentally absent. In meetings but thinking about the email I needed to send. With my family but worrying about the client relationship that was wobbling. On vacation but checking my phone every hour.

The Zero never let me fully be anywhere.

When the architecture started holding, something shifted.

I could be in a meeting and actually be there. I could be with my family and not feel the pull of the business demanding my attention. I could take a full day off and not spend it waiting for proof that I was needed.

This is what I've come to call "pressure-to-presence": the nervous system learning to trust that the architecture holds, so you don't have to.

The Return of Yourself

But the deepest return is this: you get yourself back.

Not the exhausted version who's been running on adrenaline for years. Not the hero who's defined by being needed. But the version of yourself who started this journey before it became a survival mechanism.

For me, this happened gradually. First, I noticed I was sleeping better. Then, I realised I wasn't waking up with anxiety. Then, I found myself thinking about ideas instead of problems.

And finally, one morning I sat in my backyard and realised: I wasn't just the founder of Icon anymore. I was Joe. A person with interests beyond the business. With energy for things that mattered beyond revenue.

The business hadn't needed me to be the glue for months. And instead of making me irrelevant, it made me human again.

What I Learned About Legacy

I used to think legacy was about being remembered. The company that bears your name. The success story people tell. The reputation that lasts after you're gone. I came to see that what I'd called legacy was tangled up in ego.

Real legacy, I now believe, is about building something that outlasts your adrenaline.

It's about creating an architecture that protects people when you're not in the room. That sustains culture when you're not there to model it. That makes good decisions when you're not available to decide.

Legacy is what stands after you step away. Not what requires you to stay.

I worked with a founder, let's call him John, who built a \$50M manufacturing company over thirty years. Incredible work ethic. Brilliant operator. Deeply respected in his industry.

When he tried to retire at 65, the business started falling apart within six months.

Why? Because he was the business. Every major decision went through him. Every client relationship depended on him. Every cultural behaviour was modelled by him. He'd built a monument to his personal capability. But he hadn't built architecture.

Looking at John, I saw what I'd narrowly escaped: not a legacy, but a prison of his own making.

He's 68 now. Still working fifty-hour weeks. Still the glue. Still unable to leave.

The Choice I Faced

Every leader eventually faces a choice.

You can continue to be the hero, burning bright until you burn out, leaving behind a vacuum when you finally let go.

Or you can become the Architect.

I chose to become the Architect. Not because I stopped caring about Icon's success. But because I cared enough to build something that could succeed without me. And what I discovered surprised me: building what lasts is more fulfilling than being irreplaceable.

Being irreplaceable means you can never leave. Building what lasts means you created something that gives others the freedom you fought for.

What Architecture Creates

When you build Oversight architecture into your business, here's what becomes possible:

• The business becomes an asset, not a job. You can sell it, transition it, scale it, or step away from it, because it functions independently of your daily involvement.

• The team becomes capable, not dependent. They don't wait for you to rescue them. They own outcomes, make decisions, and protect the culture because the architecture gives them clarity.

• The culture becomes systematic, not fragile. It doesn't wobble when you're not in the room. It's reinforced by rituals, protected by visibility, and sustained by distributed ownership.

• You become free, not trapped. Your value isn't measured by how

needed you are. It's measured by what you built that can grow

beyond your personal bandwidth.

This is what I built at Icon. And this is what you can build.

Not by working harder. Not by being more indispensable. But by designing architecture that makes your indispensability unnecessary.

The Architect's Legacy

The legacy you leave isn't just about the business you built.

It's about the lives you changed by building it differently.

The team members who learned to lead because you gave them ownership instead of tasks. The culture that protected people's wellbeing because you built systems instead of depending on heroics. The family you were present for because the architecture held the business when you stepped away. The future founders you might inspire by showing a different way: that you can build something significant without destroying yourself in the process.

That's what I've come to understand as the Architect's legacy. Not the company that needed you. But the system that didn't. Not the exhausted founder who finally burned out. But the Architect who built something that lasts.

The Path Forward

You now have the frameworks. The Architecture Triangle. External Calibration. The Pact. The Oversight Loop. The Drift Map.

You understand the psychology. The Weight. The Zero. The fear of empty space. The identity separation required.

You know the journey. The phases of transformation. The emotions to expect. The mistakes to avoid.

The architecture is ready.

The blueprint is in your hands.

This was the choice I faced. It's likely the choice you're facing too.

Will you continue being the hero who burns bright until burnout? Or will you become the Architect who builds what lasts?

The path is clearer than it's ever been.

And when you're ready to begin, the architecture will be waiting.

OVERSIGHT IN ACTION

Real Stories of Transformation

You've seen the architecture. You've felt the pressure it lifts. You understand the transformation it requires.

Now I want to show you how it holds for others.

The stories in these final chapters are of real founders, in real businesses, who built what I've been describing. Their names and some details have been changed, but their transformations are real. Each story follows the same arc you've been learning: from glue to Architect, from exhaustion to freedom, from holding everything to building something that holds its own weight.

CHAPTER 15

From Stagnation to Sustainable Growth

Marcus and a Manufacturing/Import Business

When Marcus first called me, I could hear it in his voice before he'd finished saying hello.

The depletion. The frustration. That particular tone founders get when they've been holding too much for too long and something's starting to crack.

He ran a manufacturing and import business, bringing specialty hardware and plumbing components from Europe and Asia, supplying trade wholesalers across three states. Forty people. Growing revenue. Multiple product lines, supply chain dependencies, the constant dance between local production and overseas sourcing. By all external measures, success.

But inside those walls, it was different.

Twenty direct reports. A flat structure that had worked when there were fifteen people, but that was now buckling under the weight of forty. His office had become a revolving door, people waiting outside, questions stacking up, decisions bottlenecked at his desk. Task boards covered the walls, every project tracked in granular detail because Marcus didn't trust anyone else to hold it.

His approach to management was hands-on in a way that suffocated.

"Let me develop your week," he'd say to his team. Then he'd write out block times for them, hour by hour, to ensure they got everything done. He genuinely believed he was helping. He couldn't understand why people were failing to perform under this system. Why couldn't they follow the plan?

His senior managers were frustrated. They'd built careers, led teams, delivered results, and now they were being asked to maintain detailed project boards for every activity. Marcus wanted visibility on everything. He was actively managing the activities, checking boxes, monitoring hours. He was more concerned about people being busy than whether they were achieving outcomes.

The harder he gripped, the worse it got.

He wasn't sleeping well. His stress was visible, in the pace of his words, in the way he talked about his team with a mixture of frustration and confusion. He couldn't understand why things weren't working. He was doing everything. Why wasn't it enough?

When we sat down, he was clear about what he wanted.

"I need you to work with my team. They're the problem. I've got good people, but something's not clicking. There's politics, confusion, projects stalling. I need you to fix it."

I listened. He laid out everything, the office dynamics, the decisions that kept landing back on him, the sales manager who couldn't seem to build systems, the projects that veered off track.

Then I said something he didn't expect.

"I'm not here to fix your team, Marcus. I'm here to work with you."

He pushed back immediately. "But they're the ones who..."

"Everything you've just described has one thing in common. You're at the centre of all of it. Before I work with anyone else, we need to look at you first."

I could see the resistance. This wasn't what he'd signed up for.

The first two months weren't about tools or systems. They were about Marcus.

He knew how to be an entrepreneur. He was a very good one. Risk-taking, self-reliance, total belief that he could make it happen, those skills had built the business from nothing.

But what we were looking at now was different: what does it take to be a CEO?

Entrepreneurial skills are about relying on yourself. Taking risks others won't take. Trusting your gut when no one else believes.

A CEO is something else entirely. A CEO works through people. A CEO trusts. A CEO inspires and coaches. They don't manage.

The very skills that made Marcus successful were now strangling the business. His self-reliance had become an inability to delegate. His hands-on approach had become a bottleneck. His "no one else can do it right" mentality had trained his team to wait for him on everything.

He had to unlearn success to grow.

We started with the Architecture Triangle and the Drift Map. The diagnostic was clear: he was the glue, over-functioning everywhere.

But Marcus didn't expect this: the work was his. Not his team's. His.

Understanding the values. Clarifying the vision. Confronting where the business needed to go, and whether he was willing to become the leader it required.

The reflection piece required humility. At one point, about six weeks in, I looked at him and said:

"I'm not sure you're up for the task."

It wasn't a tactic. I meant it. He was still resisting. Still looking for ways to make this about everyone else.

That landed differently.

But the real shift didn't happen in our sessions.

It happened at home.

Marcus came in one morning, quieter than usual. I asked what was going on.

"My wife said something last night. She asked me: 'Is this what being married looks like? All we ever discuss is the business.'"

He paused.

"She's right. I don't know how to talk about anything else anymore. I don't know how to be anything else."

That was the moment I started to see him shift. It wasn't because of anything I said. It was because he was becoming aware of his own stress levels. The Weight he was carrying. The cost it was extracting from everything that mattered.

His wife's words cut through in a way business metrics never could.

We went deeper into the values work.

Marcus thought culture was good. He pointed to the big Christmas parties, the monthly team lunches, the generous bonuses.

"I look after my people," he said.

But the Drift Map told a different story.

People were confused. They didn't know what success looked like in their roles. They didn't understand the vision beyond "grow the business." And what Marcus didn't see: they were intimidated by him.

His intensity, his presence, his way of jumping into every problem, it wasn't experienced as support. It was experienced as control.

The office politics he blamed his team for? It was a symptom of unclear accountability and people jockeying for position because no one knew where they stood.

The gap between what Marcus said his values were and how he was showing up, that was the real work.

As we started to implement the Oversight pieces, I watched Marcus closely.

Role Agreements shifted the focus from tasks to outcomes. No more "let me develop your week." No more hourly block schedules. No more project boards tracking activity for activity's sake. Instead: what does success look like in your role? What outcomes do you own? How will we know you've delivered?

The senior managers who'd been frustrated by the micromanagement finally had room to lead. They owned outcomes, not task lists.

A leadership team formed with structured reflection built in. One-on-ones moved from status updates to seeing people.

But every time we made progress, I could see Marcus get anxious. His hand would twitch toward the wheel. Old instincts screaming at him to step back in, to check, to control.

"What if they miss something?"

"What if the client is unhappy?"

"What if it falls apart?"

The Zero Principle doesn't release easily.

But something changed: by this stage, the leadership team were starting to see the drift before Marcus did.

They'd flag issues in the Oversight Loop before they became problems. They'd make decisions without waiting for his blessing. They'd own outcomes, really own them, in ways they never had before.

The architecture was holding.

The true test came six months in: a six-week holiday. Marcus and his wife, overseas. Minimal check-ins. No rescues.

He almost didn't go. The night before he left, he called me.

"What if it all falls apart while I'm gone?"

"Then we'll learn something important," I said. "But I don't think it will."

He went.

And the business thrived without his grip.

For the first time, Marcus felt the architecture holding. Problems arose, they always do, and the team handled them. Decisions got made. Clients were served. The wheels didn't come off.

He returned transformed.

The emotional detox was profound. Space felt like freedom, not failure. Silence from the office wasn't a sign of collapse, it was a sign of capability.

But the trip, while a great success, highlighted another growing phase for Marcus.

He came back relieved. The business had held. The team had performed. Everything he'd feared – collapse, chaos, clients lost – none of it had happened.

And then a different kind of discomfort set in.

"I don't know what to do with myself," he told me in our first session after he returned. "I kept waiting for the phone to ring. Kept checking emails expecting a crisis. And when nothing came... I felt lost."

This is the part no one warns you about.

When you've built your identity around being the firefighter, the problem-solver, the one who holds it all together, what happens when you're not needed in that way anymore?

Who is Marcus if he's not the glue?

So our work cycled back to him. Not the systems this time. Not the team. Him.

This was deeper than the entrepreneur-to-CEO shift. This was about repositioning who he is: his sense of purpose, his value, his identity, when he's no longer at the centre of everything.

It's uncomfortable work. The empty space that architecture creates isn't operational. It's existential.

I told Marcus: this isn't a problem to solve. It's an ongoing task. The identity work doesn't finish. It evolves.

Some days he still reaches for the wheel. Some days the old instincts flare up and he wants to jump back in. The difference now is he notices it. He pauses. He asks himself: is this the leader I want to be, or the one I used to be?

His reflection, months later:

"I spent years thinking if I wasn't in the middle of everything, I wasn't doing my job. Turns out I was the bottleneck I kept blaming everyone else for. That's hard to admit."

"Six weeks away. The business didn't fall apart. My wife and I actually talked about something other than work for the first time in years."

"I still don't know what to do with myself when there's no fire to fight. Still figuring that out."

The business grew sustainably. Revenue up. Team capability up. Marcus's hours down.

But the founder grew more, from burned out saviour to calm Architect. And he's still growing. Still learning to inhabit the space he created.

That's what the architecture makes possible. Not a business that runs. A life that fits.

And the ongoing invitation to become someone new inside it.

CHAPTER 16

Aligning Vision in a Family-Owned Food Manufacturing Company

Georgia, Mario, and a Legacy Built on Spice

In a family business, the emotional stakes are highest, because relationships and legacy are intertwined.

I didn't know that when I walked into my first meeting with Georgia. I thought I was there to review a marketing plan.

Another consultant had referred me. "They need help with their go-to-market strategy," he'd said. "Good business, family-owned, growing fast."

What I walked into was something else entirely.

Georgia was the General Manager, though that title barely captured what she actually did. Within ten minutes of sitting down with her, I watched her take three phone calls, have a quick conversation at the door with someone who "just needed a minute," and apologise twice for the interruptions.

She was polished, professional, and clearly competent. But I could see The Weight she was carrying.

When there was a pause, I asked her directly: "What's really going on here?"

She hesitated. I could see the internal battle, pride, loyalty, professionalism all telling her to keep it together, to stick to the marketing conversation.

"It's complicated," she said. "Family dynamics."

I waited.

She didn't elaborate. Her loyalty to the business, to the family, was evident. She wasn't going to air their issues to a consultant she'd only just met.

But I'd seen enough. This wasn't a marketing problem.

In our second meeting, I asked to see the owner.

Georgia led me into a back office where I met Mario, an 85-year-old Greek man with sharp eyes and a handshake that told you everything about where he'd come from.

He spoke to me partly in Greek, partly in English, and entirely in pride.

Mario had come to Australia in the 1950s with almost nothing. No English. No connections. What he had brought with him was a work ethic and a knowledge of spices he'd carried from the old country. Over decades, he'd built this business from a market stall into an extraordinary spice and food manufacturing company. Multiple product lines. National distribution. A legacy.

His pride wasn't arrogance. It was earned. Every shelf in that office, every photo on the wall, every piece of equipment in the factory, he'd built it.

When I asked him about his children and their involvement in the business, something shifted.

He turned to Georgia. She gave him a small nod, a motion that said: tell him.

"These are not my stories to tell," he said. "But I will try."

What emerged over the next hour was a picture of a family business that had outgrown its informal structure, and was now tangled in dynamics no one knew how to name.

Five grown children were involved in the business. Multiple grandchildren. Numerous nieces and nephews. All of them, in their own way, believed they were running the ship.

Harry was the eldest and the most vocal. He had opinions on everything and the confidence that came with being the firstborn son in a traditional family. But his pattern was corrosive: he'd wait for decisions to be made, then white-ant them. Undermine Georgia in side conversations. Question choices after they'd been implemented. Never direct opposition, just quiet erosion.

The "website incident" showed it perfectly.

Georgia had been charged with managing the development of a new company website. She'd spent months on it, consultations, design reviews, stakeholder input, the works. Finally, after all that work, she presented the new design to the leadership team.

And that's when Harry presented his version.

He'd been working on his own design the entire time. Never mentioned it. Never raised concerns during the process. He'd just waited until Georgia had done all the work, then unveiled his alternative in the boardroom.

The room erupted. Georgia was visibly upset, not frustrated, but wounded. Months of work. Proper process. Consultation. And Harry had simply waited in the wings to undermine it at the last moment.

This wasn't a disagreement about website design. This was a pattern. And it was destroying trust.

Everyone agreed Georgia was the glue. She held the operations together, managed the relationships, translated between generations, absorbed the tension.

But no one saw this: Georgia wasn't holding the business together. She was holding the family together. And that's a different job entirely, one that was slowly crushing her.

The work didn't start with marketing. It started with Mario, Harry, and Georgia in a room together.

We spent hours, sessions that stretched across weeks, talking about legacy.

What had Mario built? What did he want it to become? What did it mean to him to hand it over?

The conversations were intense. At times, fiery. Harry had decades of frustration he'd never fully voiced. Mario had fears he'd never admitted. Georgia had observations she'd kept to herself out of loyalty.

The business was growing. It needed leadership. The family knew there were holes, operational gaps, unclear accountability, decisions that stalled because no one knew who owned them. They were focused on these tactical matters, trying to fix symptoms.

But the real issue was underneath.

The introduction of the Oversight model helped Harry, Mario, and Georgia see a different world.

Not a world where Mario had to disappear. Not a world where Harry had to win. Not a world where Georgia had to carry everything.

A world with architecture.

We spent significant time building what would become The Pact for each family member, not defining outcomes, but understanding the motives and drivers of each family member.

Why did Harry undermine decisions? What was he fighting for?

Why did Georgia absorb everything? What did she fear would happen if she didn't?

Mario, what was keeping him from letting go?

The answer, when it finally surfaced, was simple: fear.

Mario wanted to retire. He was 85 years old. He was tired. But he was terrified that if he stepped back, everything he'd built would unravel. The business. The family. The legacy.

His grip wasn't about control. It was about protection.

Once Harry and Georgia understood this, the dynamic shifted. It wasn't their job to convince Mario to let go. It was their job to help him feel safe enough to relax.

But understanding Mario's fear didn't erase what had happened between Harry and Georgia.

In one of our sessions, I asked Harry directly: "The website. What was that about?"

He was quiet for a long time.

"I don't know," he said finally. "I told myself I was helping. That my version was better. But\..." He looked at Georgia. "I think I was trying to prove I still mattered. That I wasn't being pushed aside."

Georgia didn't respond immediately. Then: "I spent three months on that project. When you pulled out your version in the boardroom, I felt erased. Like everything I'd done meant nothing."

"I'm sorry." It was quiet, but it was real. "I didn't see it that way. But I should have."

It wasn't a dramatic reconciliation. But it was a beginning. What we built afterward had something to stand on: not just process, but the start of trust being repaired.

The Pacts we developed weren't about who owned what outcomes.

They were a framework for how this family would work together.

Clear accountability, so Harry couldn't white-ant decisions, because decisions had owners.

Defined authority, so Georgia could lead operations without needing to manage everyone's emotions.

Structured oversight, so Mario could see the business was being cared for without needing to hold it himself.

And space for legacy, explicit acknowledgement of what Mario had built and how it would be honoured as the business evolved.

The emotional cost was real.

There was grief in that room, mourning the old way, where closeness meant involvement and love meant control. The family had to learn that stepping back wasn't abandonment. That clarity wasn't coldness. That letting go wasn't loss.

Mario took an extended leave. Weeks away from the business, something he hadn't done in decades.

The business didn't just survive. It thrived.

And something else happened: the family relationships began to heal. The business was no longer the only place they related to each other, now the business was fixed.

Mario's words, months later:

"I held on so tight because I was scared of losing everything. The business. The family. All of it. Turns out the holding was what was breaking us. Now there's space. We can be family again, not just people who work together."

Georgia, finally, could lead without carrying.

Harry found his role, a real one, with real ownership, not opinions from the sidelines.

And Mario? He learned that legacy isn't about grip. It's about what continues when you let go.

The company grows aligned. But the family grew more, from entangled to liberated.

That's the deeper work of Oversight in a family business. It's not just architecture for the company. It's architecture for the relationships that built it.

CHAPTER 17

Transformation in a Critical Moment

Frank's Story of a \\$100M Revenue Company Facing Collapse

In industries where change hits hard and fast, even large companies can reach breaking points.

Frank was a CEO who led a business in traditional manufacturing, an industry where digital disruption and offshore competition had been reshaping the landscape for a decade. A hundred million dollars in annual revenue. On the surface, it looked strong: established brand, significant scale, decades of history. But beneath, cracks were spreading. Revenue was declining. Debt levels had climbed. Losses were mounting. The banks were calling in loans. Cash flow was tight. The business was bleeding.

Frank called me one day in genuine distress. "Joe, we're losing money. The banks are on my back. I don't know if we can survive this."

He wasn't looking for a turnaround consultant to "save" the business through cost-cutting or restructuring. Deep down, he knew the real issue wasn't the numbers.

It was him.

The business had grown on his vision, his drive, his hands-on leadership. He had mastered starting and scaling, the hero who made it all happen. But in crisis, those same strengths were trapping him. He was the glue: personally involved in every major decision, carrying The Weight of every failure. The Zero Principle gripped him, if the business went to zero, that zero was his alone: legacy, identity, financial security.

The emotional cost was immense: isolation, sleepless nights, fear of letting people down. His identity fused with the company: success proved worth, failure meant personal collapse.

My work with Frank wasn't about saving the business.

It was about saving the leader, so he could save the business.

We began with unflinching honesty: using the Architecture Triangle and Drift Map to reveal where he was over-functioning. The vision was clear in his head but fragmented in execution. Culture strained under pressure. Oversight was missing, he was the structure.

The deepest transformation was internal. We confronted how his hero role, once the engine of growth, had become the bottleneck. His constant intervention weakened the team. His availability created dependency. His problem-solving prevented others from stepping up.

He faced the Hero's Death: grief for the identity that built everything, fear of irrelevance if he let go. The emotional detox was raw, learning to live without adrenaline, trusting space instead of filling it.

Role Agreements redistributed weight. A strengthened leadership team owned outcomes. Renewal rhythms protected his capacity. These were non-negotiable pauses as he was so close to breaking point.

The business didn't turn around straight away. It took several months for a new rhythm to begin. But as Frank began to see his own weight – really see it – we were able to restructure the team to make the changes needed. Profitability was restored, and growth resumed. But the real transformation was in him.

He became the Architect: leading from clarity, not breaking point. Free to think strategically. Present with his family. At peace knowing the system could hold without his grip.

His reflection: "I thought I had to carry more to save the business. What I actually had to do was change. The company turned around. But honestly? The bigger shift was in me."

This is Oversight in a critical moment: when external collapse reveals the inner transformation needed. From hero exhaustion to architect freedom. Yes, the business recovers, but the real success comes when the leader is reborn.

Epilogue

The Quiet Strength of a Life That Holds

There is a moment, after The Weight has lifted, when you sit in the stillness and realise: it doesn't hurt anymore.

The tension that lived in your chest for years, that constant hum of responsibility, the low-grade panic that something was about to break, is gone. Not because the business stopped mattering. But because you finally built something that could hold itself.

I remember my moment.

It was a Sunday morning, six months after selling Icon. I was sitting in my backyard with a coffee, watching the light change through the trees. My phone was inside. I hadn't checked it in hours.

And I realised I wasn't waiting for anything.

Not waiting for a crisis to respond to. Not waiting for a decision that needed me. Not waiting for proof that I was still essential.

Just... present.

For years, I'd forgotten what that felt like. The business had consumed so much of my attention that even when I was physically away from it, my mind was still there: running scenarios, anticipating problems, rehearsing conversations.

The Oversight architecture changed that. Not by making the business perfect, but by making it capable of holding itself while I stepped back far enough to remember who I was.

What I Want You to Know

If you've read this far, you're likely carrying weight that most people around you don't understand.

The 3AM questions. The pressure that never fully releases. The loneliness of decisions only you can make. The fear, sometimes quiet, sometimes screaming, that everything you've built could fall apart.

I know that weight. I carried it for twenty years.

And I want you to know: it doesn't have to be permanent.

Not because you need to sell your business or step away completely. But because you can build architecture that holds The Weight you were never meant to carry alone.

The Oversight framework isn't about becoming less committed to what you've built. It's about becoming more strategic about how you build it.

It's about recognising that your value isn't measured by your exhaustion. That your worth isn't proven by your indispensability. That the best thing you can do for the business you love is to build something that doesn't require your constant sacrifice to survive.

The Life That Fits

I used to think success meant building the biggest business possible.

Now I think success means building a life that fits.

A life where the work matters but doesn't consume everything. Where you can be present for the people you love. Where your nervous system isn't constantly braced for the next crisis. Where you have space to think, to create, to become someone beyond the founder identity.

The architecture makes that possible.

Not by removing the challenges of leadership, those will always exist. But by creating structure that turns those challenges from overwhelming to manageable. From isolating to shared. From endless to bounded.

The Invitation

Oversight doesn't promise a world without storms.

But it builds the structure that lets you stand inside them without breaking.

If this book has done its job, it has given you more than frameworks and tools. It has given you permission.

Permission to lead without losing yourself.

Permission to step back without stepping away.

Permission to build something that serves the life you want, not just the revenue you can generate.

Permission to be a whole human being again.

You have carried enough.

The business you built deserves architecture that can hold it.

The people who work for you deserve a leader who isn't running on empty.

The people who love you deserve someone who's actually present.

And you deserve a life that doesn't require your constant sacrifice to feel meaningful.

The Framework Is Ready

The Architecture Triangle is waiting to be built.

External Calibration is available when you're ready to let someone hold the mirror.

The Pact can transform your team from task-completers to outcome-owners who bring their whole selves to the work.

The Oversight Loop can catch drift before it becomes crisis.

The Drift Map can show you where you're still the glue.

And the inner work, the Weight, the Zero, the Hero's Death, is the path through fear to freedom.

Everything you need is in these pages.

The only question is whether you're ready to build it.

A Final Word

I think often about the founders I've worked with over the years. The ones who made the shift. The ones who built the architecture. The ones who discovered, often to their surprise, that letting go of the hero role didn't diminish them: it freed them.

They're not working less hard. They're working differently. They're not caring less about their businesses. They're caring in ways that actually serve the business instead of just serving their need to feel essential.

And they're living lives that fit.

I hope you join them.

Not because I have something to sell you, although I'm here if you need help building this. But because I've seen what's possible on the other side. And I believe you deserve to experience it too.

The Weight you're carrying isn't permanent.

The architecture can hold what you were never meant to carry alone.

And when you're ready, the path is waiting.

Stand in the strength you've built: quiet, steady, and free.

Perhaps it's time to become the Architect you were always meant to be.

Appendix

The Research Behind Oversight: Data on Founder Burnout, Mental Health, and Business Impact

Throughout this book, I've referenced research on founder wellbeing and business outcomes. This appendix provides the full data, properly cited, for readers who want to understand the scope of what founders face.

The numbers are confronting. But they also confirm what you already know: you're not alone, and this isn't a character flaw.

SECTION 1: The Hidden Crisis

Mental Health, Isolation, and the Weight Founders Carry

The founder experience takes a measurable toll on mental health:

Depression and Anxiety

30% of entrepreneurs report depression, approximately three times the rate of the general population.[1]

49% of entrepreneurs report one or more mental health conditions, compared to 32% in the general population.[1]

Mental health differences directly or indirectly affect 72% of entrepreneurs.[1]

Anxiety among founders runs at more than five times the national average.[2]

Suicidal Ideation

Entrepreneurs face elevated suicide risk, with management sector professionals showing rates approximately 1.5 times higher than the general population.[3]

The isolation of leadership compounds this: most founders report having no one they can safely discuss these struggles with.

Isolation and Loneliness

76% of founders report feeling lonely, seven times the workplace average and 50% more than CEOs generally.[2]

93% of founders show signs of mental health strain.[2]

81% of founders are not open about their stressors with the people in their lives.[4]

Sleep and Physical Health

55% of founders report insomnia in the past year.[5]

53% have experienced burnout.[5]

85% report high stress levels.[5]

Founders consistently report working 50–60+ hours per week, with many in the startup phase working 60–80 hours.[6]

SECTION 2: The Relationship Cost

What Success Takes From the People Who Matter Most

The personal toll extends beyond the founder:

Relationships and Family

Divorce rates among entrepreneurs range from 43% to 48%, higher than other professional groups.[7]

Nearly half of entrepreneurs surveyed rate their romantic life as "poor."[8]

57% of business owners experiencing divorce report their company has taken a financial hit.[8]

87% of entrepreneurial couples have experienced cash flow problems that affected their relationship.[9]

Presence and Connection

Business owners are 64% more likely to prioritise business success over their romantic partners.[8]

The "always on" mentality means founders are physically present but mentally absent from family life.

70% of divorced business owners report they couldn't focus on work the same way during proceedings.[8]

SECTION 3: The Delegation Paradox

Why Founders Can't Let Go, Even When They Know They Should

The data reveals a consistent pattern:

Intervention After Delegation

Only one in four employer entrepreneurs have high levels of "Delegator talent."[10]

77% of employees say micromanagement hurts their morale.[11]

70% of employees consider leaving their jobs because of micromanagement, and 30% actually resign.[12]

Fear-Based Retention

Founders who struggle to delegate often cite fear of losing control, doubts about team skills, and concerns about quality.[13]

This fear persists even when founders intellectually know their intervention is limiting growth.

The Impact on Teams

Teams under high-intervention leaders show significantly lower ownership and engagement.[10]

High turnover from micromanagement incurs significant costs in recruitment, training, and lost productivity.

SECTION 4: The Business Impact

What Founder Dependency Costs in Dollars and Growth

The financial implications are substantial:

Valuation Discounts

Key person discounts typically range from 10–25% of enterprise value, though they can exceed this range depending on company-specific risk factors.[14]

Systematised businesses can sell for 7–8x EBITDA while founder-dependent companies struggle to reach 4x.[15]

Founder-centric businesses typically fetch 2–3x multiples; architecture-centric businesses command 5–7x or higher.

Exit Readiness

Strategic buyers often walk away entirely from founder-dependent businesses due to "key person risk."[15]

Founder dependency worsens deal terms beyond purchase price: extended earnouts, larger escrow amounts, and extensive employment agreements.[15]

Most founders planning an exit worry most about "what happens when I'm not there."

The Post-Pandemic Acceleration

Founder stress levels have risen significantly since 2019.

49% of founders say they are considering quitting their startup.[5]

Remote and hybrid work has intensified leadership challenges, with fully remote employees reporting 25% loneliness rates compared to 16% for on-site workers.[16]

A Note on These Numbers

These statistics paint a sobering picture. But they also point to something important: the struggles you face aren't personal failures. They're systemic outcomes of a role that was never designed for human sustainability.

The architecture this book describes doesn't eliminate the challenges of leadership. But it distributes the weight so you're not carrying it alone.

Citations

1\. Freeman, M.A., Staudenmaier, P.J., Zisser, M.R., & Andresen, L.A. (2018). "The prevalence and co-occurrence of psychiatric conditions among entrepreneurs and their families." Small Business Economics, Springer Nature. Published May 11, 2018. Original research: "Are Entrepreneurs Touched with Fire?" (2015), UC San Francisco/UC Berkeley.

2\. Richardson, C. (2024). "Founder Resilience Research Report 2024." Foundology/UCL School of Management, in partnership with Enterprise Educators UK. Survey of nearly 400 entrepreneurs worldwide.

3\. National Institute for Occupational Safety and Health (NIOSH). Management sector suicide rates study. Referenced in Central Valley Christian Counsel analysis (2024).

4\. Startup Snapshot (2023). Founder Wellbeing Survey. Referenced in Fintech Takes analysis.

5\. Sifted (2024). "49% of founders say they're considering quitting their startup this year." Survey of European founders, March 2024.

6\. Multiple sources including: Gallup/Gartner surveys; Karl Hughes startup analysis (2025); Penelope research on micro-business owners averaging 52 hours per week.

7\. Marriage.com/The Businesswoman Media (2023). Analysis of entrepreneur divorce rates.

8\. Clarify Capital (2024). Survey of business owners and romantic relationships. Referenced in Fortune Well, February 2024.

9\. Harp, T. Harp Family Institute research on entrepreneurial couples. Referenced in Entrepreneur magazine (2016) and Medium/Thrive Global (2018).

10\. Gallup (2014). Study of entrepreneurial talent profiles, including 143 CEOs on Inc. 500 list. "Delegating: A Huge Management Challenge for Entrepreneurs."

11\. Multiple management studies on micromanagement impact, including WorkBetterNow analysis (2025).

12\. Zoho Workplace (2024). "Micromanaging in the workplace: Challenges and tips." Management Consulted report on employee turnover due to micromanagement.

13\. Workast (2024). "Entrepreneur's Delegation Dilemma." Analysis of common delegation challenges.

14\. William Buck Australia (2025). "Assessing the impact of key person risk on business valuation." Framework for key person discount determination.

15\. Strategic Exit Advisors (2025). "Founder Dependency: The Hidden Valuation Killer That Could Cost You Millions."

16\. Gallup (2024). "State of the Global Workplace: 2024 Report." Analysis of employee loneliness by work location.

Resources

Quick Reference: The Oversight Framework

Before diving into the tools, here's a brief guide to the key concepts in this book.

The Core Problem

The Oversight Gap: The space between what you think is happening and what is actually happening. Where leaders unconsciously become the glue.

Founder as Glue: When the founder becomes the connective tissue holding everything together, creating dependency instead of capability.

Working IN vs ON: Working IN means you ARE the system. Working ON means you're BUILDING a system that doesn't need you.

The Architecture

The Architecture Triangle: The three elements every sustainable business needs: Values (vision, direction and purpose), Culture (how people behave), and Oversight (the system that connects them).

Role Agreements: Documents that define Outcome Ownership, not task lists. They include success metrics, authority boundaries, and escalation points. A critical evolution from job descriptions, but not the final step.

Human Architecture: The third pillar of Oversight. The integration of Outcome Ownership with who the person actually is, built on four layers: Personal (life outside work), Professional (career growth), Organisational (business outcomes), Cultural (values in action).

The Pact: What a Role Agreement becomes when Human Architecture is applied. A mutual commitment between founder and team member that integrates what someone owns with who they are, where they're going, and what they value.

The Oversight Loop: The operational rhythm that catches drift. Four stages: Clarity → Alignment → Accountability → Renewal.

The Drift Map: A personal diagnostic tool revealing where you're complicit in drift. Four questions examining clarity, culture, accountability, and renewal.

The Psychological Barriers

The Zero Principle: The founder's visceral fear that everything could collapse to Zero, a weight they carry alone.

The Weight: The accumulated, invisible pressure of constant responsibility that founders bear.

The Hero's Death: The necessary grief process when a founder releases their identity as the indispensable problem-solver.

Identity Separation: Distinguishing your worth as a person from the performance of your business.

The Transformation

Hero to Architect: The shift from reactive, proximity-based leadership to intentional, systematic design.

External Calibration: Using outside perspective (advisors, coaches, peers) to see what you can't see from inside.

Structural Renewal: Building rhythms that restore capacity before it's depleted, not as a reward for survival.

Tools and Next Steps

Throughout this book, I've referenced practical tools that can help you implement the Oversight architecture. Here's where to find them:

The Oversight Assessment

A diagnostic tool to identify where your architecture is strong and where drift is occurring. Use it to establish your baseline before beginning the work, and periodically to measure progress.

Available at: twoicons.com.au/assess

Build the Architecture

If the assessment confirms what you already suspect, and you want guided support through the transformation, Oversight workshops and advisory services are available. Because as this book has shown you, the hardest part is not understanding the architecture. It is becoming the Architect.

Oversight Workshops: Facilitated sessions where founders build their architecture together. Peer calibration with others who understand the journey.

Available at: twoicons.com.au/workshop

Advisory Services: For founders who want one-on-one guided support through the transformation. Work with someone trained in Oversight architecture who has walked this road.

Available at: twoicons.com.au/advisory

A Final Note

No assessment will do the internal work for you. No workshop will make the Hero's Death easier. No advisor will give you courage you have not cultivated yourself.

The architecture is yours to build.

When you are ready, the path is waiting.

Acknowledgements

This book exists because of the people who lived it with me.

To my daughters – Rebecca, Renee, and Ellie – you're already in the dedication, but you deserve to be here too. You saw the cost. You stayed anyway.

To Cathy, who was there for the journey. The weight of building Icon wasn't mine alone to carry.

To the Icon team, past and present – Paula, Sheree, Andy, Nicole, Erica, Janene, Lozzy and the many others who gave years to what we built together – you carried more than I asked and forgave more than I deserved. What we built together taught me everything in these pages.

To Wayne, the consultant who sat across from me in 2015 and told me the truth I didn't want to hear. You planted the seed. It just took me years to let it grow.

To Lindley, whose mentorship shaped how I think about leadership long before I had the language for it. Your influence runs through these pages more than you know.

To Clinton, who saw the numbers tell the story before I could. Your steady hand through growth, COVID, and the sale gave me the clarity to see what needed to change.

To John and Armin, who met and prayed with me every Wednesday morning for many years. You held space when I couldn't hold myself.

To Dave and Tom, my dear mates who trained with me – whose business ethos made for moments of incredible laughter, irreverent wisdom, and lasting friendship.

To the clients whose stories appear in this book – thank you for trusting me with your businesses and allowing me to share what we learned together.

And to Kat, my editor, who took a manuscript full of hard-won lessons and shaped it into something others might actually want to read.

Finally, to God – the backbone of this journey. When The Weight was too much to carry alone, faith held what I could not. That foundation continues to lead and anchor my life.

This book is mine. But it belongs to all of you.

About the Author

Joe Papadatos graduated from the University of Technology Sydney in 1989 with a Bachelor of Applied Science in Applied Chemistry. But it wasn't the lab that called him – it was the boardroom. He began his career at Unilever and National Starch and Chemical, where he found his feet in their global sales and marketing teams, rising into senior roles and developing the structured thinking that would later shape his approach to business.

It was his time working alongside John and Ken at Western Graphics that opened his eyes to the realities of small business – the weight founders carry, the gaps they fill, and the pressure that never quite lets up.

In 2003, Joe founded Icon Visual Marketing from a lounge room in Southwest Sydney. Over the next twenty years, he transformed it into the region's largest marketing agency, growing the team to more than forty people and serving clients ranging from SMEs to national brands and local councils.

Along the way, Joe worked with hundreds of founders. Not household names, but the SMEs and family businesses that form the backbone of the Australian economy. He watched them struggle with the same pattern he would eventually recognise in himself: businesses that succeeded because of their founder's involvement, but couldn't thrive without it.

In 2023, Joe sold Icon to an international agency. After twenty years of being the glue, he was ready to build something different. That transition – and the rebuilding that followed – became the foundation for the OVERSIGHT framework.

Today, Joe is the founder of Two Icons Consulting, where he works directly with founders of 10–100 person businesses who are ready to stop being the system and start building one. His approach integrates sales, marketing, operations, and leadership into a coherent architecture that holds under pressure.

Joe lives in Sydney.